Reuen Thomas

Divine Sovereignty and Other Sermons

Reuen Thomas

Divine Sovereignty and Other Sermons

ISBN/EAN: 9783337114565

Printed in Europe, USA, Canada, Australia, Japan

Cover: Foto ©Lupo / pixelio.de

More available books at **www.hansebooks.com**

DIVINE SOVEREIGNTY

AND OTHER SERMONS,

BY

REUEN THOMAS,

MINISTER OF HARVARD CHURCH, BROOKLINE.

Author of "Emmanuel Church," etc.

BOSTON:
D. LOTHROP & COMPANY,
FRANKLIN AND HAWLEY STS.

LONDON: JAMES CLARKE & CO., FLEET ST.

PREFACE.

I have been many times asked, by friends in England and America, to publish a volume of Sermons, but have hitherto refrained because I was not conscious of anything specially new in my way of presenting Biblical truth; and because my method of sermonizing, being a mixture of the prepared and extemporaneous, is of all methods least fitted to do itself credit in print.

These sermons that I now offer to my friends and the public have not been re-written for publication, but are given, as nearly as possible, as spoken from the pulpit. The first six were a brief course to inquirers; intended to be suggestive and expository, not at all controversial. The other sermons are ordinary Sunday morning discourses.   R. T.

CONTENTS.

I.—Divine Sovereignty	7
II.—Man's Sinfulness and Inability	20
III.—Atonement and Expiation	35
IV.—The Divine Helper	49
V.—The Witnessing Church	62
VI.—Retribution	74
VII.—Means and Ends	88
VIII.—"Worship God"	102
IX.—The Child and His Dues	118
X.—A More Excellent Way	136
XI.—The Pre-eminence of Christ	148
XII.—Our Relationships	163
XIII.—The Limitations of Evil	179
XIV.—For His Name's Sake	194
XV.—Searchings of Heart	210

XVI.—The Divine Responsibility	223
XVII.—Predestination	235
XVIII.—Self-Improvement	250
XIX.—Weariness in Well-Doing	264
XX.—The Divine Invisibility	279

I.

DIVINE SOVEREIGNTY.

And Jesus came unto them and spake unto them, saying, All authority hath been given unto me in heaven and on earth. Go ye therefore and make disciples of all the nations, baptising them in the name of the Father and of the Son and of the Holy Ghost: teaching them to observe all things whatsoever I commanded you; and lo, I am with you alway even unto the end of the world.— *Matt.*, xxviii: 18.

THE words "Divine Sovereignty" have oftentimes been so used as to create a prejudice against them. Man's own ideas of Sovereignty have been imported into them. I am aware that in using them I may put myself at a disadvantage in obtaining, with some, ready receptivity for the ideas which I propose to ask you to consider. Persuaded as I am that many of these ideas have not been correctly apprehended or adequately appreciated,— persuaded also that there is in them truth so important that if we let it slip, we shall suffer in increased mental imbecility and moral feebleness, it seems to me to be my duty to speak to those of you whose minds are open to the truth which Jesus the Christ has brought within our grasp, on these essential things — not theologically or dogmatically but exegetically and ethically.

The Christian Church, through its Apostles, received originally a commission from its Founder.

The record runs thus: — "The eleven disciples went into Galilee unto the mountain where Jesus had appointed them. And Jesus came unto them and spake unto them, saying, All authority hath been given unto me in heaven and on earth. Go ye therefore and make disciples of all the nations, baptising them in the name of the Father and of the Son and of the Holy Ghost: teaching them to observe all things whatsoever I commanded you; and lo, I am with you alway even unto the end of the world."

This is a sweeping statement. It speaks of authority — of authority as deposited in a person. It suggests that that person has in himself the substance of the Divine nature — otherwise the formula to be used in baptism is unintelligible. His apostles were to go forth to make disciples of all the nations. They were to administer disciples' baptism. They were to put the *name*, which implies the ownership of God, on those who were baptised. They were to declare, thus, that they belonged to God. They were to declare that the nations belonged to God. In a word they were to announce and maintain the Divine Sovereignty over nations. That Divine Sovereignty for this world is deposited in Jesus the Christ.

This is the truth that underlies all else in the commission given to the disciples. *Therefore*, because all authority hath been given unto me in heaven and on earth, go and make disciples of all the nations.

We must not *limit* the authority and think of it as confined to the church or to Christians alone, and to them only so far as they are members of organized Christian societies — and only to their acts as members of such societies. There is no such limitation in the words of our Lord. "All" cannot mean less than " all. " The moment we begin to limit revealed truths by man's opinions that moment we begin the process of belittling everything which Jesus has spoken. That moment we begin the exaltation of man over Christ — that moment we enter on a course the exact opposite of the one suggested by John the Baptist: "He must increase but I must decrease." We are not " of the truth" when we set up the opinions of men as of more worth than the explicit teachings of Christ.

Authority—all *authority*—all Sovereignty over man is vested in Christ.

We can see reasons why it should be. On the

ground of knowledge; He knows more of the nature of Deity — more of the nature of man — and more of the nature of things than any other who has ever been on this earth knows.

On the ground of goodness; He has submitted himself to all the tests to which the nature of man can be subjected and has triumphed in all. Tried and tempted by every form of evil, he remains the sinless one — spotlessly good.

But goodness is not simply abstinence from acts of sin or feelings that are sinful. It is not merely negative. It is positive. This Jesus Christ has done everything possible to be done by any human, or as far as we can see, by any divine being for the sake of helping others. He has loved the Eternal Father with all his heart and his neighbor as himself.

That is all I feel called upon to assert, at this present stage, on the nature of the goodness of Christ. On the grounds of knowledge and goodness, in a word on the ground of the superiority and excellency of his nature, he is Sovereign. It is according to all that we know or imagine of the Divine Nature that Sovereignty should be deposited in him who is greatest and best.

In the superiority and excellency of the nature of Christ we may see a practically sufficient reason why the Divine Government of mankind should be *administered through Jesus Christ.*

It is not to be wondered at that in the ultmate ordering of the Divine Government *superiorities* should be invested with authority.

In this age we are compelled to search for the *ground of things.* We must dig down to that which is fundamental. There is too much lawlessness in society to allow of serious men putting one set of opinions against another and in angry faction fights contending that one set of opinions is right because it is old, and another set wrong because there is the flush of youth about them. As a general principle we may assume that whatever has stood the test of age has essential truth in it. The seemingly new must expect to be regarded with suspicion until its worth has been tested. Whoever accepts an opinion simply because it is new and for no other reason stamps himself as frivolous. But oftentimes it happens that that which seems to be new is the oldest of all. A new machine is often the bringing of principles which are as old as the Universe into more effective operation. Nothing really new is introduced. The old is brought into a neater useableness. When the lightning shall have been domesticated and made to light the girl who has to sew into the weary hours of night, nothing new will have been brought into the world. It will only be a more perfect understanding of the old. Everything new in all departments when proved practical and useful is simply more perfect understanding of the old. Let us put away all fear of knowledge. Ignorance is the thing to be feared — ignorance of God — ignorance of ourselves — ignorance of the world in which we live. That the ignorant people of the country should practically rule it — being the multitude, and having votes to cast for those who represent themselves, this is the danger. And it is much more of a danger than any of us see. It was ignorance which crucified Jesus the Christ; "Father, forgive them, for they *know not* what they do."

The Church of Christ must beware of narrowing its mission to the world within any limits more contracted than those assigned to it in its original commission. We have to proclaim the Sovereignty of God in an age when so many are proclaiming the sovereignty of man — i. e. the sovereignty of the multitude — let that multitude be composed of whomsoever it may. It is true, as one has said, that the idea of modern democracy has become predominant under the influence of the preaching of the truths which, in their best expression, are in the New Testament. "Heathenism had no such notion of man as man; it had no glimmer of the preciousness of a soul; it had no likeness to this, introduced and diffused in the western world, which revealed that it is not for the high, nor for the philosophical, not for the wealthy, not for emperors or nobles or patricians of Rome, but that it is for man as man, for each soul of man that God has sent His Son to shed his blood, and sent his Spirit for renewal and restoration to himself as to a Father's bosom." But you have to choose between the Democracies — a Christianized democracy or a demonized democracy. In all its history the Church of Christ has never been in the position in which it finds itself to-day, here, on this continent. And I am afraid we do not see the peculiarity of the position and therefore the duty of the hour. I fear that we ourselves are only half awake to our responsibilities in regard to organized society. Have we any definite idea of the Kingship of Christ in reference to society? Has not this very idea of the real Sovereignty over man, as man, being deposited in Christ, a feeling of unreality about it? Do we see that if it be a truth it is the most practical of all truths? When a man takes Jesus as Christ he takes him as his Sovereign — not simply as his Prophet, his Teacher — not simply as his Priest — but also as his King. He has to take him for all he is, or he can never rise to the full stature of a man in Christ Jesus.

The questions of most urgent practical importance in our day are such as relate not to freedom but to Government, to Sovereignty, to Authority, to Law and Order. There are some countries in which the duty of the hour would be to speak of Freedom, its nature and its necessity. There is no such duty laid upon us in this century so far as this country is concerned. In order to have right ideas of freedom we must first of all have right ideas of Sovereignty. If we understand the prophetic element in the New Testament Scriptures rightly, the development of the spirit of lawlessness is to be one of the signs of the latter days of the present dispensation of things. I am fully aware that the effect of preaching the fulness of the Divine nature — that in which the gospel consists — that God is love — will be in some minds, to produce laxity. And yet for the sake of those who have a right to all that is revealed of the Divine Nature we must not withold any truth. What we need to see is that Love works through law and not independently of it. God is light as well as love. The word light suggests holiness. It suggests purity. It suggests intelligence. It suggests wisdom. All the beneficences of the Universe depend upon law. Destroy law and what then? Then chaos and destruction. Love is seen to demand for its sphere of operation law and order. These are the ideas we need to have impressed upon our minds in this age.

What is the foundation of *human law?* Is there

such a thing as authority? What is it? On what does it rest? In what is it rooted? What is the ground of it? We must ask these questions and we must find answers to them. Without debating the matter I venture the affirmation that there is no answer to be found *outside religious truth*. An irreligious man may say, 'It is necessary. It is expedient.' But why? 'We cannot make our fortunes — we cannot possess our comfortable and luxurious homes — we cannot sleep well at nights — we cannot pursue our pleasures quietly, without law and order.' But supposing the great multitude should be instructed enough in our public schools, just enough, to lose all that natural fear of superiorities which belongs to superstition and ignorance; supposing they should listen to the men who represent lawlessness — the men who have nothing to lose even if society becomes a chaos — what would they care about these material things on which we place so much value? Considerations of necessity and expediency would go for nothing. If there be no Divine Sovereignty — in itself righteous — with the *right* to rule, with the right of authority, then all these lower sovereignties are usurpations. Everything that man has is *derived*. From what source is the authority which is invested, for instance, in the President of the United States; in the Governor of this state; in the Judges of the supreme court; in Judges everywhere — derived? Has it any right to be? The Christian man, if he is as intelligent as Christianity is capable of making him, has his answer ready. And it is all-sufficient. It is this — 'There is a Divine Order in this Universe. The Creator must be the Sovereign by right and in fact. We have nothing which is not derived. Not a faculty, not a power but is derived. We are not independent. All round and all through we are dependent. We are born into an established order of things; an element in it; a part of it. We do not stand alone — cannot stand alone. We are related all round.' There are no facts less open to question than these — that we are related to certain institutions — the family and the nation — yea, the Kingdom of Christ, for it existed as revealed in the family and nation into which we were born. We are thus related to organisms which God has made. We are thus related to Him. We are under the Divine Sovereignty. There can be no doubt of it. Our accepting it or rejecting it does not alter the fact. We are in the midst of a system of laws which God has established. We cannot get from under them. They are in us. We are organized in accord with them. Thus the Sovereignty of God comes into our very nature and makes it what it is. These dependencies and these relationships put upon us duties and responsibilities.

Herein comes our freedom — we may intelligently and voluntarily work with God (to the measure to which He has revealed Himself) in the family, in the church, in the nation, or we may ignorantly and wilfully (all we can) work against Him. In the one case we are subjects, in the other rebels. In the one case we rise into the condition and feeling and apprehension of children in a household, and are as free and happy as children at home; in the other case rebellion gradually but surely hardens down into that wilfulness which becomes, in the process of time, total alienation moving steadily toward demonism. The facts of life compel us to see that irreligion never stops at mere inhumanity. Its final form is demonism.

Now, the irreligious man has no answer to the question — on what rests the authority which is vested in the parent in regard to his child; in the Governor in regard to the State; in the Judge as regards the administration of law? When I say that he has no answer, I mean that he has no answer which is not like a house built on the sand.

If an eternal foundation for a temporal institution cannot be found it cannot stand; it must go. All permanent necessary institutions have their ultimate authority in the right of the Creator to govern — in a word, in Divine Sovereignty. Democracy may be so regarded as to become the hugest idolatry which has ever been set up in the world — the idolatry of the will of man. The Christian can have nothing to do with it under that aspect. God's ultimate purpose in reference to nations is declared to us in that nation of Israel. That ultimate purpose is not democracy but theocracy — not the rule of the many over the few, but the rule of God over all. And if the Church of Christ fails of seeing this, and of teaching it, and of illustrating it in its own life — it so far fails of comprehending the greatness of the commission entrusted to it, and the basis truth on which that commission rests. All rightful authority over man is deposited in Jesus the Christ. He is the sole Sovereign. To submit to his Sovereignty is to be in right relations with God, and so, essentially, to be free from guilt. To refuse to acknowledge that Sovereignty is to be out of rightful relations towards God, and so, to be now and as long as the refusal continues, guilty in God's sight. And while the Creator has revealed himself as "long-suffering, plenteous in goodness and truth — not willing that any should perish but that all should come to repentance," yet has he also said that "he will by no means clear the guilty." Let us try to appreciate something of the magnitude of this most practical and most necessary revelation — "All authority hath been given to me in heaven and on earth, go ye therefore and make disciples of all the nations, baptizing them in the name of the Father and of the Son and of the Holy Spirit : teaching them to observe all things whatsoever I commanded you; and lo, I am with you alway even unto the end of the world."

II.

MAN'S SINFULNESS AND INABILITY.

All have sinned and fall short of the glory of God.—Romans, iii : 23.

IN speaking on the theme of Man's Sinfulness and consequent Inability I am not under the necessity of occupying your time in any elaborate attempt at proving either the one or the other. It is universally admitted that there is something defective, inharmonious and wrong in man's nature. The best and the worst of men admit this much. Any man who argued to the contrary would be regarded as lacking in intelligence as well as in moral sense, as odd and singular, as a man whose views and opinions of things were so peculiar as to cause him to be regarded with something of suspicion. In every one of us there is a something good which perceives a something bad and wrong. There is also something in every man which whispers of an ideal state. There is in all a kind of reminiscence of a lost condition. This reminiscence has never, I think, been more exquisitely phrased, than in the poet's Wordsworth's "Intimations of Immortality from Recollections of Early Childhood." The poet can account for the inward condition which he finds in himself and in other men only by the suggestion that we have had a prior existence, traces of which still remain with us:

> "Our birth is but a sleep and a forgetting;
>   The soul that rises with us, our life's star,
> Hath had elsewhere its setting,
>   And cometh from afar;
> Not in entire forgetfulness,
> And not in utter nakedness,
> But trailing clouds of glory do we come
> From God, who is our home."

In order to account for what we find in ourselves we need not accept the extreme explanation of the poet. It suffices if we think of our nature as having had, originally controlling it, a supreme love which has been largely but by no means entirely lost, which is now only a reminiscence. The idea of the lost condition hides itself in the soul but can never "except in the worst of the worst" be entirely killed out. That in us which accuses us when we do wrong and commends us when we do right cannot be fallen and sinful. *That* must be righteous and holy. And so there is in us all a viceroy asserting Kingship in the name of the true Sovereign of our souls. Job recognized it. David recognized it. Call it Conscience, call it what you will, it is there as a fact.

And I am dealing, in the simplest possible way, with facts of consciousness.

But there is in us not only this sense of righteousness — of a lost ideal state but much else. In every man there is *a sense of incongruity* — of dividedness of nature — of disharmony. We are not at one with ourselves. The Apostle Paul puts the case thus — "The flesh lusteth against the spirit and the spirit against the flesh, and these are contrary the one to the other." There is a depravity, a degeneration in our nature. And as the several parts of our nature are so intimately associated that if one part suffers all the other parts suffer with it, so the depraved condition is not moral alone or intellectual alone, or physical alone. All departments are weakened from their original strength, and corrupted from their original purity. The intellect, the affection, the will, are not in that condition which is seen to be possible. As a matter of fact we look upon one another as beings not entirely trustworthy. Every man puts every other man upon trial, and does not entirely trust him until he has had considerable experience of him. If man be not a depraved creature, why this universal suspicion? Surely no one would choose to live in a perpetual state of distrust, for it is an exceedingly uncomfortable state. And yet, the men and women who are naturally at the farthest remove from this suspiciousness of disposition, are compelled by the experience they have of life to exercise no little of caution. Without parading the acknowledged vices of society before your gaze, there is enough of evidence among the most decent and well-behaved people of the world to testify that we have in us the conviction that all men everywhere are in a depraved condition. And yet they are not so depraved as not to know that they are depraved.

It is often argued that we are here in a state of probation. But man as man has had his probation and has fallen. It would seem that innocence apart from experience cannot stand. The representation of the case in the Book of Genesis is that Adam's "tree of knowledge of good and evil" tested his obedience. Our Tree of Life — Jesus Christ — tests our obedience. Only with a difference. The first man of whom we read, knowing only good, wanted to know what evil was. We, having in ourselves the knowledge of good and evil, are put upon trial, whether we will adhere persistently to that which is good — not simply good in the abstract — good only as an idea — but good in the concrete — good personalized in Christ Jesus. Nothing appeals to our whole nature until it becomes personalized.

Taking these simple facts, which are undeniable, — what does this condition mean? Is there any explanation of it? There is suggested the explanation of *incompleteness*. Our nature, say some, is moving on gradually towards unity, harmony, perfection. Give it time and it will come out according to the highest idea that the best and most intelligent man has of it. Theoretically this looks plausible. And if we could shut ourselves away from ourselves, and from all the facts of society, the idea of simple imperfection might seem large enough to cover the case. The apple is green and tart, but leave it alone for a month or two, and it will be pleasant to the eye for its color, and sweet to the taste. Unhappily, except under certain conditions, and in a certain environment, man as he grows older does not grow better. The generosity, the trustingness, beauty and sweetness of youth, seem to fade away, and nothing quite so good comes in the place of them. In most cases the whole of this life of ours seems to be occupied with the scattering of illusions; with the proving that our views are short-sighted; that our opinions are false; that our pleasures cannot last; that the things which seem to be blessings are very often curses in disguise, so far as their relation to individuals is concerned, and worst illusion of all, that which relates to our own view of our own nature. There is something else than incompleteness. This idea does not account for our sense of guilt — a sense belonging to every man — the most pitiable form of misery, and yet, strange to say, the deepest possible sense of guilt is not half so appalling as would be no sense of it at all. Whether the restlessness and the superabundant activity of the world are not more due to the inward sense of guilt in man, from which, in one way or another he is striving to free himself, than to anything higher, is a question worth while our considering. "The wicked is like the troubled sea which cannot rest, whose waters cast up mire and dirt. There is no peace, saith my God, to the wicked." The idea of incompleteness as accounting for what we find in ourselves is not large enough. It leaves out too much. There are too many facts which lie outside of it.

It covers a part of the ground but only a part. It needs along with it the idea of *depravation* — an idea which satisfies the Conscience as well as the Intelligence. The sense of not being right — of being wrong — of being at war with something — with SOMEONE, is in us all. This is what we call the sense of sin. This sense is not consistent with inward happiness. It is an internal trouble which men would get away from if they could. But no man can get away from himself. He may change his place of abode — his associations — his surroundings, and for the time be so occupied with the newness that presents itself, as to get a partial and temporary relief. But the old internal state is there, and soon re-asserts itself in all its power.

No external condition can eradicate it. Men try all sorts of devices to rid themselves of this internal sense of something wrong. Sometimes they change their opinions, putting off one set, and adopting another. But the taking up with that which is more lax, or that which is more thorough, does not alter the inward condition. The bad consciousness is there all the time. It is deeper in the nature than the region to which opinion belongs. It is not wrong opinion simply but something more inward which troubles us. There is on other word but sinfulness which will express the nature of the trouble. We have from the past inherited a depravity — a degeneration of nature. And it has corrupted the intellect — the affections — the will. We think wrongly — we feel wrongly — we act wrongly. And we are all in the same state. No man can set himself up as of a different order of being from the rest. "God be merciful to me a sinner"— is a prayer suited to everyone.

While I am carefully abstaining from the use of scientific theological expressions, and interpreting the simple facts of consciousness, yet I can find no word that will stand in the place of this word 'sinfulness.' For it is quite certain that there are in man not only defects which mean weakness, but that there is also a parent defect which means guilt. There is no man living who has not this sense of inward guiltiness. And those who, to us, seem the best and the truest are the readiest to acknowledge that it belongs to themselves equally with others. So generally is this the case, that the claim of perfectionism, on the part of any, is met with a general incredulity not unmixed with scorn. The man is suspected all the more because of his claim. It seems to be indecent as well as impossible. Apart then from the gross vices of the disreputable among men and women, we perceive that there is, in this nature of ours, a degeneration which is not simply a defect, not simply an entrenched ignorance, but a condition so radical that all efforts of self upon self are insufficient for the freeing of our nature from it.

And *this degeneration is total*—by which I mean, it affects the whole nature. No part is untainted. It is not possible that any part should be. Our nature is so connected, part with part, that degeneration in one region means degeneration in every region. If a man be unjust in his feelings he will be unjust in his thinking and unjust in his action. It is the merest rubbish to talk of a man being good at heart and bad everywhere else. If the fruit of the tree be bad the tree is bad. And sinfulness means corrupted feeling, corrupted thinking, corrupted willing, corrupted action. The unity of our nature necessitates this. Great thinkers in all times, and in all countries, have perceived that if that centre we call the heart be depraved all other parts of our nature are lowered thereby. In his Ethics the old Pagan philosopher Aristotle writes " For depravity perverts the vision and causes it to be deceived on the principles of action, so that it is clearly impossible for a person who is not good to be wise or prudent." " The pure heart makes a clear head" says another of the ancient celebrities. So Carlyle in modern times, to quote only one of many, writing of Mirabeau asserts, " The real quality of our insight, how justly and thoroughly we shall comprehend the nature of a thing, especially of a human thing, depends on our patience, our fairness, lovingness, what strength soever we have; intellect comes from the whole man, as it is the light that enlightens the whole man."

Let us bear in mind this, then, that whatever affects the centre of our nature affects also every part of it to the outermost extremities. If there be impure blood in the heart there will be impure blood in every vein of every part of the whole body. And so, if there be depravity in the affectional region of our nature there will be depravity in the will region, in the region of the intellect, in the action. Nothing will be what it would be if that depravity were not there. I want that our young people especially should recognize that a degenerated heart means a degenerated intellect.

This degeneration means not only bad disposition, it means biassed and depraved intellectual quality, inability everywhere. And this must of necessity be so, because of the unity of our nature. So that on the highest themes, the thinking of a man out of right relations to God is not trustworthy, cannot be, nor on any themes which involve character. To say that there is no difference in the moral quality of opinions, and that one set of opinions is as good as another, is surely to speak so as to draw away from us the intellectual respect of all thinking men. There is more depravity in one set of opinions than in another. There are some views of man's nature and of life which make it much easier for a man to sin than other views. Now I do not think that there is any mercy, or any kindness, in any teaching which leads men to assume that sinfulness is only an eruption on the skin and not a disease of the heart. Only "fools make a mock at sin." There are countless instances of men so coarse and vulgar in feeling, so far away from all true refinement of mind, that, seemingly, they have no perception of sinfulness as a spiritual malady. Until it externalizes itself in vice, until it shows itself in acts of degradation and shamefulness, they do not recognize it as of any consequence. They take no note of the disposition to folly and stupidity which belongs to the depraved condition; no note of the terrible moral torpidity which belongs to it. Sinfulness when it becomes vice, disease in the body, destruction of tissue, spoliation of form, making loathesome that which God made beautiful — that is the only aspect in which sin stirs their natures into any feeling of antipathy. And even over that they can jest.

I venture the assertion that anyone who has mind and heart great enough to look under the surface of things, and not simply at the outside of things, must perceive that there is sin *and* sin. Do we not make a distinction in our own feeling between sin which indicates infirmity and sin which indicates a self-assertive determination to do and be something which involves pride, envy, malignity and the utmost of want of consideration for others? The New Testament speaks of " sins of the flesh " and " sins of the spirit. " The devil sins, we must remember, were not committed in the flesh, and yet they are of all sins the most heinous.

Now it cannot be doubted that the view we take of this fact of sinfulness, universally admitted in some form, will influence our estimate of every other vital truth. If sinfulness be only ignorance we need only a Teacher. If sinfulness be only the inward condition which has gradually been wrought in us from our misconception of things, we need only an Instructor. If sinfulness be only disease we need only a Physician. If sinfulness be only error we need only an Example. But if it be something more than ignorance, something more than disease, something more than error, we need in Him who is to deliver us from it a power other than that possessed by the Teacher, the Physician, the Exemplar, as I believe that the New Testament distinctly teaches. If I were to occupy myself in trying to make you believe that the sinfulness in this nature of ours can be swept out by any amount of education of the intellect, by any degree of culture, however thorough, which stops short of the culture of the heart, I should be false to the deepest convictions of my nature. And whatever comes of it I must be true to these; and especially so when I think that others may be misled by my underestimating of how much is involved in this word 'sinfulness.' Sinfulness means ignorance, yes; it means error, yes; it means disease, yes; but it means a great deal more. In many and many a case it means that state of heart in which the idea of God is more hateful than the idea of the Devil. I look upon those who are vicious, the fallen man, the fallen woman, the drunkard, the libertine, the debauchee, and it is sad enough, God knows. But I have known fallen men and fallen women and drunkards who have never from their youth up ceased from praying 'God be merciful to me a sinner.' I do not want to forget the lines of the hymnist :

> "Think gently of the erring one!
> And let us not forget
> However darkly stained by sin,
> He is our brother yet.
>
> * * * * * * * *
>
> Heir of the same inheritance,
> Child of the self-same God;
> He hath but stumbled in the path,
> We have in weakness trod."

I want to live in that spirit and temper of mind as long as life shall last. I dare not trust my own short-sighted views of sin. On all these questions I want to be a learner from Him who is of all Teachers on vital matters incomparably the greatest. I cannot forget his words spoken to men whose place in the society of his day was not the lowest — "The publicans and harlots enter the Kingdom of God before you." There are sins of the flesh which pollute, which destroy reputation, which bring wretchedness and misery, social degradation and much else. There are sins of the spirit which bring none of these, and yet, if Jesus of Nazareth be a true prophet, which put men and women at even a farther distance from God. The teaching is not mine, it is His. Of what condition of heart is he who is amiable and placid until someone speaks to him such a truth as is contained in these words 'God is Love. God is Light. God so loved the world that he gave His only begotten Son that whosoever believeth in Him should not perish but have everlasting life." Then, his whole soul is filled with aversion to the speaker, with wrath, with disdain. To err is human. But to gnash with the teeth when the claims of Deity are put before the mind, that is not human. It is not simply inhuman, it is *fiendish*. I hate the word, but I am obliged to use it. No one has ever taken a true measure of what sinfulness is until he has considered it in this, its most terrible form.

And yet even at this stage of it, we need not hang our heads in despair. I am no advocate of that shallow theology which is simply a formulating of the opinions of sinful fallible men. I hope that God will keep me from the insufferable conceitedness which denies that which transcends my very finite understanding. I have no wish to be frivolous or to help any of you to a capability of jesting in this charnel house of corruption into which we have been looking. I want you to feel more than ever you have done "the exceeding sinfulness of sin," for only then will you be able to appreciate the exceeding goodness of God who "willeth not the death of a sinner but that all should come to repentance."

"Where sin abounded grace did superabound."

No man who looks away from his sin to his Saviour need despair, but then he must look to him as Saviour, not simply as Teacher, not simply as Exemplar, not simply as Physician, as the strong Son of God, the only personalized power stronger than sin itself. "When the strong man armed keepeth his palace his goods are at peace, but when a stronger than he cometh upon him, he taketh away that wherein he trusteth and divideth his spoils." If a man can grow out of this condition of sinfulness by natural development; if every highly-cultured man be an unsinning man; if every old man be nearer to the ideal of manhood than when he was young; if these be facts and experiences everywhere met with; then a Teacher, a Physician, an example, is needed; but if otherwise, if it be seen that man acting on himself, is helpless to free himself, helpless to deliver himself from the presence and power of sinfulness, and from the inward sense of guiltiness, then he who is to meet the necessities of the case, must be human to understand him, but more than human to redeem and deliver him from an enemy stronger than man himself.

III.

ATONEMENT AND EXPIATION.

But this man, after he had offered one sacrifice for sins, for ever, sat down on the right hand of God.—*Hebrews*, x: 12.

OUR theme this morning is Atonement and Expiation. I could not satisfy my sense of reverence for that which is peculiarly sacred, if I should enter upon our brief consideration of the thoughts suggested by these words *controversially*. In days when so many religious people have given over sober and steady thinking, and have taken to dogmatizing, it becomes pastors to *feed* their sheep, not to set the dog of controversy at them. In order to vigor of body there must, in each of us, be a good steady appetite for wholesome and nutritious food. And so likewise in order to vigor of mind and heart, there must be a good steady appetite for such *truths*, as tend to enlarge the mind, and such facts, as tend to vitalize the heart. Let us not be scared at names and words which to many have been made odious by being used as party watchwords only. Our duty is to try to understand what they mean. Do they stand for a *truth*? Not simply for an *opinion*. An opinion is the product of a man's mind; a truth is the product of the Divine mind. It is in accord with the nature of things. Opinions change all the time. Truth never changes. Our little systems have their day and cease to be. Truth is not of a day, or an age, it is from eternity to eternity. Our apprehensions of it may change — *will* change if we *grow* at all — but the change will be, not from larger to smaller, but from less to more. The change from larger apprehensions to smaller indicates moral deterioration. The change from less to more indicates spiritual growth.

These words " atonement " and " expiation " have become party words. Consequently many persons have never taken the trouble to try to understand them. But the man or woman who in religion is a mere party man or woman is certain to be so full of prejudice that he will shut out much truth which his soul needs. That condition of mind is not fair nor honest. The man who is sincere, open, candid, wants to know the truth as far as the limitations of the present time will allow. Consequently, he is always a disciple, always a learner, becomes assured of some things — feels the ground under his feet firm as far as he has gone — but is still moving onward and upward. He is a growing man all the time, and the sign of growth is an increasing humility, that is an increasing teachableness, which amounts to the same thing as perpetual youthfulness of spirit. He never becomes hardened in intellect or fossilized in heart. Life is full of interest because of the immense area which is still unknown. "At the best, our knowledge is but a little island floating on and amid an infinite sea of mystery." After all, it is the mystery which lies all around the little we know which makes our life so unspeakably interesting. I am thankful that that which I do not know is so immeasurably more than that which I know. I am thankful that I am only at the beginning of things. I am thankful for the ability of recognizing that this life is only a life of beginnings, that we know nothing yet in any other than a rudimentary way.

If this be true of life as it is in the lowest organism, how much more of the life of man, the highest organism of which we know anything? Tennyson plucks the little flower out of the crannied wall, and as he holds it in his finger, addresses it in this way: —

> "Flower in the crannied wall,
> I pluck you out of the crannies;
> Hold you here, root and all, in my hand,
> Little flower — but if I could understand
> What you are, root and all, and all in all,
> I should know what God and man is."

If there be no rhapsody, no exaggeration there, if the little poem be only the ornate dressing up of a simple true thought, what shall we say when speaking of great facts concerning our own life, such facts as these which come to us in these two words — " Atonement and Expiation " — words, let me say, more for the heart than the intellect? I adopt as my own, the language of a thoughtful speaker and say — "If, as we believe, Christ is both God and the Son of God ; (and to suppose any being less than God perfectly manifesting forth God, is a contradiction,) if moreover he is Man as well as God, and if this Son of God and Man has made a sacrifice, in virtue of which the sin of the whole world is taken away (so far as God himself is concerned), then surely the Atonement effected by this mysterious person must itself be a mystery, the full import of which we cannot hope to fathom. No man however wise, or learned, or devout, should affect to comprehend it; no man whatever his attainments, should venture to speak of it save with modesty and reverence, and with a profound conviction that he knows it " but in part," that he sees it but as " through a glass, darkly." I adopt this language as my own. It exactly expresses my own feelings. Atonement is not a New Testament word. It belongs specially to the Old Jewish dispensation. It is represented by a Hebrew word which means to cover up. When the old Hebrew did that which was appointed to put himself into right relations towards God — when he offered the sacrifice which meant that his will was to do God's will, then he was said to be atoned — that is, brought into oneness with God. In the sacrifice offered, he regarded himself, his blood, that is to say his life, as offered in consecration to God. He knew, however, that this sacrifice had no meaning in itself. It stood for another great sacrifice which one day should be offered, a perfect sacrifice, the sacrifice of a spotless and sinless one who should be his representative, who should do for him what he could not do for himself. But this symbolic act of sacrifice of his did something for his heart and conscience, which required to be done. The devout Israelite could not rest until he had done something to indicate that he was not willingly a rebel against God. His heart was pained, his conscience was uneasy, so long as he had not performed an act which indicated the sorrow of his soul, and the submission of his will. The mere general proclamation that God was merciful and gracious, was not enough. If only Jehovah had himself appointed something to be done, how gladly would he do it, if only He had declared that there was some deed, the doing of which, indicated that He was *at one* with the man who had sinned, and the man *at one* with Him, how gladly would the devout Israelite do it. And so, in answer to the necessities of this nature of ours, Jehovah appointed a sacrifice which at one and the same time, should be prophetic and expiatory. The devout Israelite offered the appointed sacrifice — it satisfied his heart, it appeased his conscience, and he went to his home rejoicing that he was at peace with God.

I want that we should note these simple things: — 1st, that the sacrifice offered was required by the necessities of this nature of ours, which is never satisfied by a mere declaration apart from an act. "Lord what wilt thou have me to *do*?" was the cry of the awakened soul. "What shall I *do* to be saved?" was the question of the aroused jailor of Philippi. This is human nature all the world over. And they who affirm that a man's soul ought to be satisfied by mere inferences as to the nature of Deity, by mere inferences as to the mercy of God, can never have sufficiently considered what human nature is. No soul but the meanest could be satisfied with a mere verbal declaration of this nature —" I forgive you, but I don't want to have anything to do with you." The little child in the household would teach us a better theology than that. If the father says, " I forgive you" and then coolly turns his back on the child, is it satisfied, does it feel the forgiveness? Does it realize it? No; it realizes it when the father puts his arms around its neck, and the child its arms around the father's neck, and the kisses of the father bring the tears. There must be an *act* of forgiveness as well as *words* of forgiveness, or our nature is not satisfied. And all theories to the contrary proceed on a very shallow and inadequate apprehension of what human nature is. The heart and conscience of the devout Israelite demanded some act which breathed forgiveness, but more than forgiveness — restoration to communion — and the act of sacrifice was both these.

2nd, I want that we should notice further that the act must be an *appointed one*. It must indicate God's will, not the self-will of a sinner. Self-will is the root of all sin. And so, even an act of worship which indicated the perpetuation of self-will would only be a continuation of rebellion. That is the explanation of the difference in the acts of the first two men of whom we ever read as offering sacrifice, Cain and Abel? Abel's offering is represented as being acceptable, that of Cain as not acceptable. Why? Abel offered that which was appointed to be offered. Cain offered what he chose. The one man honored the will of God as supreme, the other honored his own will. We can never understand an act until we get down to the principle which is in it. When the sinning man has done the *appointed* thing, then the heart and conscience are satisfied; they are assured, because God himself has appointed the act. There is no satisfaction to heart and conscience where there is no assurance.

Remembering these two ideas, we can have no very serious difficulty as to the meaning of sacrifices in the Old Testament times. The Creator knew the necessities of our nature better than the theorists know them, and he met those necessities in the appointment of the mosiac sacrifices.

But human nature is the same now as then. It is conscious of sinfulness. The consciousness is always a troublesome one; it may even be acutely painful; yea, it may become positively agonizing. It has never been satisfactory to any but torpid souls to issue simple, general declarations of the Divine mercifulness. And, especially, when mercifulness is made to mean easy good nature, which does not much discern the difference between good and evil, and does not much care for the difference. Any man who thinks, perceives that on this earth the most selfish, the most useless, and the most unreliable people in any community. are these easy good-natured people who don't care how things go, so that they are not disturbed. To take the idea of mercifulness which belongs to these, and transfer it to God, is to give men a Deity for which the most earnest among them cannot feel even respect. Men have in them the intuition that the nature of God must contain, that which is represented to us by the words, Justice and Righteousness. They have an intuition that He cannot be man's enemy, for He preserves him in life, and loads him with benefits. They have also a distinct recognition that a Righteous Being — a Just Being, cannot move down from his Righteousness and Justice — cannot compromise it, cannot be ashamed of it, can do nothing to deny it. He must be at unity with Himself. Abraham felt all this when he exclaimed, "Shall not the Judge of all the earth do *right*. Job felt it when he said, "I know that my Redeemer liveth." Paul, too, when he exclaimed, "Let God be true though every man be a liar."

The question forces itself upon every *earnest* man's soul, sooner or later — How shall this Righteous, this Holy God, who cannot change from his holiness, be still just, and yet enter into fellowship with his men and women who are all confessedly sinners and rebels? He loves their humanity, for he is the Author of it. But He is, and must ever be, at war with their sinfulness. There is the problem. It is too deep for you and me. Man has free-will. It cannot be forced. How shall God and man be made one again? We cannot look into the profundities of this question. The theories of the theologians as to Atonement and Expiation all fall short of a full explanation. That being so, is it not wise to take the simple revealed facts, and leave the theories alone. No one but He who can look into human life, and all life, as it is from the beginning of the Creation, till now, and on endlessly; no one but He who can see our relation to other beings, and other worlds, *can* fathom the theme. But Scripture has taught me this — and I am sure that I have been willing to learn; I am sure that I have been willing to have no opinions of my own, and no views that might intercept my clear recognition of what it does teach, it has taught me that it was *necessary* that Jesus should offer Himself as a sacrifice in order that He might deliver us from "the captivities of evil." It was *necessary* that Jesus should offer Himself as a sacrifice in order that the government of God should be so administered that there might be no stain on the Divine purity, and yet the man who turns Godward might have full and free pardon and deliverance from the evil which is in him, and its consequences. It has taught me that it was *necessary* that Jesus the Christ should put Himself at the head of our humanity and be its Representative and do for us completely and perfectly what we can do only in a very imperfect and rudimentary way.

It has taught me that He came not to alter the will of God — not to set it aside — but perfectly to do it — and that no one but Jesus *has* done that will perfectly on this earth. It has taught me, that when the Eternal Father of our Spirit, saw his will perfectly done on this Earth, He made the One who did it the custodian of all who could *not* do it — gave them into his hand — made them his possession and his heritage — and so we are Christ's. We belong to Him. We are his people. And neither can the sins of this world slay our immortal spirits, nor can the terrors of the dark side of the other world touch our real life, if we cling to Him. That much Scripture has taught me. And my heart is satisfied. My conscience is satisfied. And if my intellect refuses to be satisfied I don't care. It has never yet been satisfied and probably never will be — because we can know only in part.

But the intellectual light of to-day will disappear before the intellectual light of to-morrow, as the stars disappear when the sun rises, swallowed up in the brighter light. Man is not all intellect. There is something more precious in him than intellect, although this proud, haughty part of his nature, like an ill-bred and unrefined man, is ever asserting itself as supreme. Religious teaching, which is simply addressed to the intellectual in man, may make disputants and controversialists and conceited sectarians, " ever learning and never coming to the knowledge of the truth," but in order to wake the whole of our nature into healthy life, we need no diminished Christ, no Christ reduced to the stature of a fallen man, a man who was not here yesterday and will not be here tomorrow. We need something else than a candle, yea, than a thousand candles of man's manufacture, if we are to make the flowers grow in our gardens, the trees to be bright with foliage, and heavy with fruitage, we need the full orbed Sun. And so too, if we are to have in our churches, Christian men and Christian women, not simply religious controversalists and religious wranglers, we need the full-orbed Christ; He who spake, as never man spake, to the Intellect; He who whispered to the Conscience and it ceased its upbraidings; He, who in the might of His unbending integrity, stood before Pilate and Herod the world's Judges, and even they found no fault in Him; He, who on Calvary, mutely appealed as none other ever did or ever will to the human heart, and that heart wept in penitence and joy and gladness. For we cannot refuse to recognize this, that those who think only of the Sacrifice which Jesus made of Himself as a manifestation of the Love of God, may only too easily come to rely on that Love without responding to it. In that case, so far as the individual is concerned, the greatest of all facts ever revealed to the human mind is outside of us. It is something looked at, not appropriated. Every unappropriated good necessarily becomes a condemnation. The soul, not capable of responding with its love to God's love, is in a lost state *now*, and must, by whatsoever discipline and affliction God may send, be brought into another state before it can see the Kingdom of God.

I do not wonder that the great soul of the Apostle of the Gentiles should test the condition of every man by this simple but all-sufficient test. Does the love of his heart respond to the wondrous love which Jesus has shown towards men? I do not wonder that the holy indignation within him should glow and burn until it voiced itself in these words, "If any man love not the Lord Jesus Christ, *let him be Anathema!*"

You and I, brethren, need not concern ourselves about Adam and his sin, and its consequences, *that* is all done and done with. The question for each man, to whom the gospel of the grace of God is preached, is this, "why is there no loving response in my heart to the love which is in Christ to me?" If there be one truth taught in the New Testament more clearly and more frequently than another, it seems to me to be this — that Jesus Christ came into this world to put away sin by the sacrifice of himself. Is it not enough? Is it not what we need? In this turbulent world, this world of strife, this world of bitter enemies and false friends, this world of uncertainty and change, this world in which we know not what a day may bring forth, this world in which so many prefer the fellowship of devils to the fellowship of God and good men, it must surely be a necessity for the heart to have some centre where it can rest and find peace. For if the heart be at rest the man is strong and brave in trials and afflictions which ruffle the outside. That centre is given us in Him who has taught us all of our Father God we know. And it seems to me our true attitude is that expressed in the words of the hymn:—

> "My faith would lay her hand
>   On that dear head of thine,
> While like a penitent I stand
>   And there confess my sin.
>
> My soul looks back to see
>   The burdens thou did'st bear,
> When hanging on the accursed tree,
>   And trusts her guilt was there.
>
> Believing, we rejoice
>   To see the curse remove;
> We bless the Lamb with cheerful voice
>   And sing his bleeding love."

IV.

THE DIVINE HELPER.

And I will pray the Father, and he shall give you another Comforter, that He may abide with you for ever.— *John*, xiv: 16.

OUR thoughts this morning are all contained in the one thought of the "Divine Helper." In speaking within such limitations as are forced upon me, I have preferred that general title, for the Holy Spirit of God to others, because it keeps closer to the meaning of the original word, than any other. The word used by the Apostle John, to designate this Divine Helper, is translated both in the Authorized and Revised Versions of the New Testament as *Comforter*. Literally the word means "One called alongside for help." Bearing in mind that this is the radical idea, I propose to ask your attention to a few considerations which may be of some practical service to inquiring minds. Only suggestions can be made. A long course of sermons would be necessary for anything like a respectful expounding of the Scriptures, which bear on this theme. And even then the dimly perceived but unspeakable would still be the greater. For, in order to growth in knowledge, and growth in spirituality, we have to force our proud intellectuality to its knees — yea, if in true Eastern fashion, it lies prone on the earth biting the dust, the attitude is far more becoming than that of erect self-willed ignorance with its innocent absurdity, "I don't believe in anything that I cannot understand," the only fitting reply to which innocent absurdity is, "Then you believe nothing at all, not even your own existence, for most assuredly you do not understand it." When the nature of that Source of life, from which all spiritual life comes is the theme, we bow our heads and listen to anyone who can teach us as much as we are capable of receiving, and there is but One who is competent to teach us authoritatively. If we have humility enough to sit at His feet, and learn of Him, we shall eventually arrive at such perceptions as are necessary to enable us to live a life of practical Christian usefulness. That is all that our God requires from us.

The first thing we have to recognize, when we think on a theme of this kind, is that man *has* a body and *is* a spirit. Therefore he is capable of thought on spiritual things — things above the material. If he were not a spirit, he would not be capable of such thought. As the Rev. E. H. Sears, in his helpful book, "The Fourth Gospel the Heart of Christ," says, "Man is natural and supernatural. By his natural organs he is placed in open and necessary relations with time and space. By his immortal faculties he is placed in necessary relations with a supersensible world. * * * All men have intuitive notions of spiritual and Divine things. Into every soul comes an influx of the supernatural, and breathings from the Lord which are deeper than all human teachings, and without which all human teachings were in vain. Were it not for these inspirations, the eternal life might as well be preached to trees and animals as to human beings." We have to recognize that we are taught from within as well as from without. We have to recognize clearly and distinctly that our life is not self-originated and self-derived — that we are not independent, but dependent beings — that we live because it is God's will that we should live — that underneath our mind, supporting and sustaining it, is the Divine Mind — that our personality needs to account for it another personality — that thus our life is permissive and not entirely or chiefly in our own keeping. These truths have to be recognized before we can touch this theme. Now, would it not be an altogether strange and unaccountable thing if the Author of our Being had so closed it up that He could gain no entrance to it? Would it not be a strange thing if He had so made us as that we could really exist altogether cut off from Him? Would not that indicate that He made us in sport? That we were mere toys, to be thrown aside after a while? That He created us for some other reason than that we might hold fellowship with Himself, and enter into the uses, and joys, and delights of His Universe? Would not the Creator have voluntarily destroyed the unity of his Creation if he had made us so that we could exist independently of Himself? In the light of these and such like considerations the revealed facts of inspiration and spiritual influence become not probable simply, but necessary.

The idea of the olden time, "There is a spirit in man and the inspiration of the Almighty giveth him understanding," is in agreement with what we see must be.

Now when in the development of revelation as given us in the Scriptures, we find a Trinity in the Godhead, it naturally starts discussion and debate, because at first it seems to militate against the idea of the Unity of the Godhead. And that idea seems to us very necessary and very precious if we are to be kept from going in the old heathen direction of polytheism. But the more we think of it the more we perceive that a mere solitary oneness is not unity. Unity implies and demands something of variety. The unity of our own nature demands it; the unity of Creation demands it. The idea of Trinity in Unity disturbs us. And so, instead of accepting the fact, and cultivating a modesty and reverence which forbids us to dogmatize on facts beyond our reach, we begin to try and get the fact put into some form in which we can understand it. And so in time, human speculations and opinions come to occupy the place of Divine Revelation.

I acknowledge that it is natural for men to reason and argue and speculate and form opinions. A living mind is full of movement and activity. And the movement and activity within it are sufficiently accounted for only by the recognition of a Power external to the mind moving it. Does it not, however, become us to recognize that great spiritual truths, which out-measure the capacity of all human minds, have never originated in them and are not to be explored by them? And no controversies have been more useless, certainly none more irreverent, than those in which mere debaters have occupied themselves in settling the nature of that Trinity which is revealed as in the Godhead of the Creator.

I do not propose to be drawn into this theme as a controversalist. My business is very simple — to make such suggestions as shall help inquirers. In prosecuting that business, I would ask you to recognize that the human mind needs for its own satisfaction the revelation of an Original Source of Life, corresponding in its powers to that which is objectively infinite. It needs that that Original Source of Life should so limit itself that it can be known.

It needs further that being known under limitations, it should still be able to so distribute itself that all can be visited, directed, helped. There cannot be any doubt of this triune necessity. Is it not provided for, in the revelation of the nature of Godhead — in the three terms used as expressing Deity, Father, Son, and Holy Spirit?

I admit that there can be no analogies in the material creation to illustrate this great fact. Material nature is too unelastic, too stiff, too formal to be used in this connection. And yet is there not something which looks towards this truth in what we know of *light?* Men sometimes have thought that they had the laugh on the old historian and legislator, Moses, because in the book of Genesis the record intimates that light was created before there was any sun in the heavens. Accordingly all superficial minds, from Voltaire, the genius of sarcasm, down to many of the knowing youths of our own day, have made merry over this remarkably ignorant old world hero. Unfortunately, however, for Voltaire and those of his disposition and temper, science patiently marching on from fact to fact, has eventually arrived at the conviction that light is in its nature entirely independent of the sun. "It is a vibration of the ether in which the sun is in our time, no doubt, the chief agent, but which may be produced by the action of many causes." And so of other discoveries which tend to show that Moses knew what Science has only recently found out. How he knew it is a question to which we wait for an answer.

Now take these facts about light. First, it was diffused, then gathered up, as far as our world is concerned, into the sun, and yet, by the sun, it is distributed everywhere, so that every flower gets its portion and every spring blossom is what it is in beauty and fragrance because of the influence upon it, of an orb more than ninety millions of miles away. To my mind there is something in this fact which looks as though it might be used to help us in our thought on this theme. I do not call it a simile or metaphor or any kind of an illustration, only a helpful suggestion in the region of material things.

Still, if it be a fact of our every day life, a fact so common as to lose its wonderfulness to all but the most reflective and thoughtful minds, that every tiny bud and flower all through the earth is what it is because of the influence on it of an orb more than ninety millions of miles away, are we asking you to receive anything absurd, anything impossible or improbable, when we aver that it is revealed that every soul of man everywhere, owes its best thoughts, its purest impulses, its noblest aspirations to the influences of the Spirit of God upon it? And as personality in man demands and proves personality in God, so these influences of the Spirit of God upon the soul are personal. They are such influences as a person produces on a person. Silent as the light, they are none the less powerful because of their silentness. In the quietude of the soul that Holy Spirit of God is operating, as our Lord taught us, convincing of Sin, of Righteousness, of Judgment, creating within us, that is to say, a sense of Sin, a sense of Righteousness, a sense too that the present order of things is not to last forever, that there is a period when the great decision will be made, that there shall not continuously be this present confusion of Sin and Righteousness, of Truth and Falsehood, the Bad often lauding it over the Good. There is in us all a sense that this cannot last, that it must come to an end. And this sense of sin in us, this sense of Righteousness, this feeling that there must be a judgment which shall reveal and deliver, is the sign of the action of the Holy Spirit of God on our spirits.

Who of us does not see how much of dignity

and worth is added to this life of ours by this revelation that the spirit of man is ever open to the influences of the Holy Spirit of God? Why can man think thoughts that never occur to an animal? Why can he write books like Milton's Paradise Lost, Dante's De Coelo et Inferno, that wondrous book of Job, those ever-inspiring Psalms of David, Tennyson's In Memoriam, Longfellow's Psalm of Life, uncounted volumes on a life above the material life? Because he is a spirit. Because being a spirit, the push of the Eternal Spirit is ever on his, moving him, stirring him into thought and feeling, making him aspire, suggesting prayer, which is only devout aspiration. This is why. We all of us have done our best to sink into the animal life and find our satisfaction there and have failed. We have failed because our God would not let us succeed. By the influences of His Holy Spirit He has been brooding over us, moving in us, keeping our conscience in life, stirring up our feelings. The reason why the sap in all the trees is being vitalized just now and sending out bud and leaf, is because the beams of the sun are in more energetic operation within. And the reason why any of us have at any time been stirred into religious thought, and devout aspiration, is because the energetic influences of the Spirit of God have gained access to our minds and hearts. The light has been poured into us from an unseen hand. It is because of the undying energy of this Holy Spirit of God that we have any devout thoughts, any filial feelings Godward, any disposition to pray, any delight in praise, any faith Christward, any love to our fellow-men. It is not *our* doing; it is *His*. "Not by might, nor by power, but by my Spirit, saith the Lord." What have we that we have not *received?* What have we originated? Nothing but sin. Everything else has its root in the Holy Spirit of God. Our ability of perceiving that Jesus is the Christ of God is of God. No man can call Jesus Lord, but by the Holy Spirit. Of all gifts of God, this practically is the greatest. There is nothing good in human nature that is not traceable to it.

Now, this era in which we live, is peculiarly the dispensation of the Spirit. The New Testament seems to indicate that while there is a general, what we may be allowed to call a natural, creating and sustaining energy of the Spirit of God, for all men, in all places and times, according to their ability of receiving it, there is in this era since the coming into this world's life of the Christ of God a much more copious exercise of Divine energy upon the soul of man, so much so that " where sin abounded, grace did much more abound." No one can doubt this, that since the advent of the One who stands before us as God's Christ, the world has had new energy in it, new movement, new life, purer ambition, loftier aspiration. That "power from on high" which was promised to the Apostles of Christianity, and which made itself specially felt at Pentecost, was not an exceptional gift to them. It belongs to all who could receive it. I believe that we should understand this truth more if we were less self-dependent and less dependent on material things, than we ever can understand it in the present condition of society. The greatest as well as the best man, is he who has the largest receptivity. An Apostle speaks of the old man and the new man. The new man is the Christian man. The old man is the mere selfish materialist, the man who is the centre and circumference of his own world. When a man is brought to act from new motives, new principles, and aims at a new and higher life, when his own birth and death are not the bounds of his horizon, but he perceives the necessity for Eternity in order to develop the larger life which is in him, and of which he is conscious, is he not a new man? Is it not clear that he is born from above? There is nothing in the flesh to account for these new views and aspirations. There is nothing in the animal to suggest to his mind the spiritual. There is nothing in the finite to suggest the infinite. Why has he these thoughts and feelings, these cravings and aspirations, these dissatisfied longings, these soarings beyond and above the terrestrial? He has them because of the visitings to his Spirit of the Holy Spirit of God. And if he does not yield to them, if he resists them, if he puts them among dreams, if he tries to rid himself of them, if he goes into societies where nothing of them will be recognized, if he exercises himself in the opposite of these, doing everything he can to materialize and sensualize his mind, he is fighting against God; to use Apostolic speech he is *grieving* the Spirit of God, he is trying to put out the fire lit within him; he is doing what in him lies to " quench the Spirit." Thus the case is represented to us by our Lord and His Apostles.

Their teaching explains to us the meaning of our inward dissatisfactions. This nature of ours must ever be a problem to us, " the flesh lusting against the Spirit and the Spirit against the flesh," a problem insoluble until we recognize that the nature of God is round about us, that " in Him we live, and move, and have our being," as much and as really as the flowers and birds live, and move, and have their being in the sun-impregnated atmosphere. Then we begin to understand why conscience will not rest, why the heart within us is not at peace, why the mind cannot be kept from thinking, why unsyllabled prayers move noiselessly within our souls. It is the voice of the Holy Spirit within saying to us, "This is not your rest; there remaineth a rest for the people of God."

That which M. de Laveleye has written of society in general is true of every individual life: "There is in human affairs one order which is the best. That order is not always the one which exists; but it is the order which should exist for the greatest good of humanity. God knows it and wills it; man's duty it is to discover and establish it."

V.

THE WITNESSING CHURCH.

Which is his body, the fulness of him that filleth all in all.—Ephesians, i: 23.

THE questions, what is a Christian church? what its relation to the Christ from whom it takes its name? what the conditions of membership in it? what its relation to society in general, and all such questions, have to be answered in the light of the Person and work of Him who is its Head. The Church is called the body of Christ. Through his body a man holds communication with the outer world and works in and on that outer world. So through His church Jesus the Christ acts upon society, upon men in general. I do not say that this is the only medium through which He works and acts, but it is the principal medium. A church, then, must be organically fitted to express the mind and will of Christ. Every thing ecclesiastical which is not so fitted is an encumbrance, a hindrance, and not a help.

So far as any church expresses only the mind of man in any age or generation, so far it is defective. Ecclesiastical constitutions exist in which our Lord has no direct and immediate influence. There is so much put between Him and His church that His aspect to the members must be like that of a man at the small end of an inverted telescope. Everything which comes between the soul of man and the Christ which is not transparent, yea, which has not in it the power of bringing this Christ nearer to the soul, is so much hindrance to a human spirit in its strivings Godward.

In inquiring as to the nature of the Church of Christ, the following ideas demand recognition:—

1. Christ Jesus is its head; its sole head, its source of doctrine, of law and of order. He only has authority. "One is your Master even Christ, and all ye are brethren."

Of course in every society there must be a head. Even a mob must have a leader. There must in every society be law and order. Otherwise there can be no peace and no progress. The self-will of the individual becomes everything. And in such a state of things there can be no co-operated movement. The simpler any organization is the more catholic it is, and the more competent for the highest ends. The sole headship of Christ in the Church is the basis doctrine of all law and order. That headship was distinctly acknowledged by the Apostles. Passages from the Gospels and Epistles might be quoted if it were necessary, to prove how jealously this headship was guarded, both by our Lord himself and by his Apostles. " No servant can serve two masters," is our Lord's warning to those who would try the experiment of a double allegiance.

In the Epistle to the Romans, St. Paul almost indignantly repudiates the idea of one member of the church claiming authority over another when he asks: "Who art thou that judgest another man's servant? To his own master he standeth or falleth." In the light of such passages as these, it is strange that such abuses as exist should have crept into the ecclesiastical world. Lordship in the Church, says Wycliffe, is forbidden, brotherhood is commanded. I know of nothing of more practical importance than that we should never forget that Headship and Authority in the Church are vested in One and in One only. Let us not abuse the idea by inferring that there is no Authority, and that men can do in the church as the whim takes them. Nothing could be farther from the truth of things than such an inference. There are law and order in the Church, but the law is not derived from man, and the order is not such as he has instituted. Therefore is the law so sacred and the order so impressive. Its very simplicity may mislead us; not having our eyes open to perceive that the simplest ideas are parental, that they contain in them no end of fruitful and legitimate applications. There cannot be room for a doubt, that our Lord, in giving two sacraments, and in instituting a ministry, intended a visible Church on earth. There can be as little room for doubt that He intended that the acknowledgment of His sole headship over them, should be the first and chief sign of membership in that church. The man who has no ability of owning the mastership of any one but himself and his own will, has no place and can have no place in the Christian Church. He is self-excluded.

If we are willing to submit to be taught by Christ, to be guided by Him, to be controlled by Him, we are of his Church. That willingness is God's call in us. And whatever special experiences we may have or may not have, they are entirely unreliable, entirely deceitful indeed, if we have not that willingness. Having that willingness however inexperienced we may be, however uninstructed, however spiritually dull and incapable, or however richly endowed with the capacity of spiritual perception, we are without doubt under the influences of the Spirit of God and are of that numberless number who constitute the church of Christ. Let me say plainly that genuine self-depreciation is no disqualification for membership in the church of Christ; rather is it of the nature of qualification; the consciousness of "not being good enough," is no disqualification but otherwise; if that feeling be genuine and not assumed, it is an element in self-knowledge. The feeling 'I shall never be able to be consistent' is no disqualification, or the whole membership would have to step down and out. Christ is able to keep us from falling away from Himself, and that is the crucial thing. Our ability is not self-derived, it is imparted. Willingness to be led and guided, and saved from sin and its consequences by Him who is the Head of the Church — this is the essential thing in qualification. Without this willingness we have no place and no right in the Church of Christ.

2. The membership of the Church is a brotherhood. If we have the ability of the subordination of our own wills to the will of Christ, the practical result will be, that we shall be of the same feeling and disposition as all others dowered with the same ability. The spirit of brotherhood will be in us. For when anything of the love of God enters the heart, the love of man comes with it. The one is the result and the sign of the other. And the love of man is not some sentimental feeling which is here to day and gone tomorrow. It is that disposition which shows itself in sympathy and goodwill, which is pained when it

pains others, which seeks to be united with others in all such acts of generous helpfulness as are feasible. It is the diametric opposite of the spirit of judgment and accusation. It takes note of the Master's words, "Judge not that ye be not judged; condemn not that ye be not condemned." When circumstances forbid it to do good it resolutely refuses to do evil to any man. If it can find a good motive for an action it refuses to believe in a bad one. It seeks to be in unity with all who in sincerity submit to our Lord Jesus Christ. It is ever mindful of the Savior's prayer, "That they all may be one as thou, Father, art in me and I in thee, that they may be one in us, that the world may know that thou has sent me." To be brothers of all who will have us for brothers, brothers of all "who name the name of Christ and depart from iniquity," this is the aim, the hope, the ambition of the true Christian. Our minds and hearts need society. God has so constituted us that we cannot stand alone. The individual as an individual is not God's idea of man but the individual in family relationships. We know this because God has made family relationship necessary to the perpetuation of the human race. Yea, he speaks of the church as a family, "Of whom the whole family in heaven and earth is named." So a disciple of Christ standing apart in his individualism is not God's idea of a Christian, but a disciple in the family, one of many. "Members of one body, every act of separation and self-will, is an offence against that body and against its head." "One is your master, even Christ, and all ye are brethen," this brief sentence covers the whole ground. All else in practical church life is included in, and derived from, these two abilities, the ability of the subordination of our own self-will to the will of Christ, and the ability of persistent untiring brotherliness in speech and conduct.

It is necessary to add that the members of the Church of Christ are called by other names than this of "brethren." This indicates the tone and temper of their minds. They are called "believers" and "disciples," which words indicate their standing towards their Lord. They are called "saints," that is, separated ones, which word implies that they refuse to be controlled by the world's ideas and fashions, whenever those ideas and fashions militate against the simplicity and sincerity of their allegiance to Christ. It is necessary to add further that the Church of Christ is not democratic, but theocratic. The people are not the fountain of law and order. They have no right to affirm who shall be the head of the Church; that is settled — settled forever. Nor have they any right to say what truths shall be taught, and what doctrines affirmed; that also is settled and settled forever. The Church of Christ is a witnessing church. "Ye are my witnesses," saith the Lord. "Thus it is written that the Christ should suffer, and rise again from the dead the third day; and that repentance and remission of sins should be preached in his name unto all the nations, beginning from Jerusalem. And ye are witnesses of these things." This from St. Luke. And again in the beginning of the Acts of the Apostles: "But ye shall receive power, when the Holy Ghost is come upon you, and ye shall be my witnesses both in Jerusalem and in all Judea and Samaria and unto the uttermost parts of the earth."

The Church of Christ is not charged with creating or inventing anything. It has to be the witness to the facts and truths revealed concerning God and man in and through Jesus Christ. It is charged with the grand and glorious responsibility of taking these revealed facts and truths to all who bear the name of man, from one end of the earth to the other. For God Almighty never gives a man a truth for his own private use. Every revealed truth belongs to the whole humanity. Wherever the sun shines there it is God's will that His revealed truth should shine. It is necessary that we should distinctly recognize that though these facts and truths may suggest views, and start opinions in men's minds, yet that those views and opinions are not the foundation on which the Church is built. Other foundation can no man lay than that is laid, Jesus Christ. Endless confusion has arisen in the ecclesiastical world from a non-recognition of the distinction between men's views and opinions on the facts and truths of Holy Writ, and the facts and truths themselves. However many sects and denominations you may have, there is but one Church of Christ. However multitudinous the views and opinions of men on religious themes, there is but "one Lord, one faith, one baptism, one God and Father of all, who is above all, and through all, and in you all." The Church derives its facts and truths, its law and order from Christ, not from the people — it is theocratic, not democratic.

This also must be added, that the church is the dwelling place of the Holy Spirit of God, which fact is evidence by these fruits of the Spirit which hang thick and threefold upon it, as upon a tree of life. "The fruits of the Spirit are love, joy, peace, long-suffering, kindness, goodness, faithfulness, meekness, temperance (or self-control.)" These abound in every true Christian Church.

We must not omit to add, that the Church is Christ's great Teacher to the nations. The last great command to the Apostles runs thus: "Go ye and make disciples of all the *nations,* baptizing them into the name of the Father and of the Son and of the Holy Ghost; teaching them to observe all things whatsoever I commanded you; and lo, I am with you alway, even unto the end of the world." If the Church abdicates this position, or does not recognize it, it lives outside its commission and opportunity. I venture to say that there is no other power adequate to educate the mind of a nation or a man. I need not remind you how far short of its opportunity and commission the Church of Christ has fallen, when we take into consideration its relation, not only to individuals, but to nations. The truth of the Gospel has even been so used as to promote selfishness. Many a man has been taught that the beginning, middle, and end of Christianity is to save his own soul. Of course that is the beginning of Christianity, but it is not the middle and end. When once a man has been brought into right relations toward God, by the acceptation of Jesus Christ as his Redeemer, Lord, and Master, practically he is brought into new relations towards men. He begins to recognize that he owes duties to the family, and to the nation. He begins to feel the misery and meanness of a life which lives to get and not to give. His eyes are opened to see that this is the kind of life most antagonistic towards the life of God. The parasite on the tree which drains away its life but adds nothing to the life of the tree, is the fit symbol of the man who gets everything out of the nation he lives in, and gives back nothing so far as his own will and purpose is set to do it. The Church's commission includes the teachership of the nation in all highest things pertaining to national life.

And lastly, the church is the beginning of that permanent society which God is organizing to embody and express his will. The Book of the Revelation of St John gives intimations of a perfected society into which there enters nothing that defileth, neither that which believeth or maketh a lie, a society of the pure and true, or rather of those who are purified and made true, men from all ages and all nations, all kindreds and all tongues, a society of men like in sympathy and disposition though various in many other ways. The Christ of God is the centre of that society; its inspiration; its archetype; a society based on inward character not on anything else, the inward character being attested by outward allegiance to this Christ of God. In that society we shall get the perfection of communion, the ideal fellowship, all lovelessness gone, no envy there, no hatred, nothing that leads to schism, no insincere man there, no unbrotherly man, the society of which the church on earth has been, in its best estate, only the promise and prefiguration. John the Divine saw it in vision, and he wrote " Behold the tabernacle of God is with men and he shall dwell with them, and they shall be his people, and God Himself shall be with them, and be their God. And he shall wipe away every tear from their eyes; and death shall be no more; neither shall there be mourning, nor crying, nor pain any more; the first things are passed away."

"And there shall be no curse any more; and the Throne of God and of the Lamb shall be therein; and his servants shall do him service; and they shall see his face, and his name shall be in their foreheads. And there shall be night no more; and they need no light of lamp, nor light of the Sun, for the Lord God shall give them light, and they shall reign forever and ever."

VI.
RETRIBUTION.

Be not deceived; God is not mocked; for whatsoever a man soweth, that shall he also reap.—*Galatians*, vi: 7.

THE fact of Retribution is necessarily a very serious one to all who are not "past feeling." We find the law of retribution working here in our life. It cannot be denied. The natural inference is that a law here indicates a similar law beyond the period and condition we call temporal. Ostrich-like, we may hide our heads in the sand and refuse to see that which is disagreeable. It is wiser and better always to face facts, never to ignore them, never to close our eyes to them. Interrogate them. Ask them what they mean and what they have to teach. Let us take what we *do* know and let it lead us to inferences consistent with it as to that which we do *not* know. Let us have the courage resolutely to stand by the laws and facts which are revealed.

We recognize in ourselves, and so in other men, a sense of a righteousness which ought to be obeyed and maintained; and we recognize also a condition of feeling, mind, will, life, that is not according to righteousness. All our efforts to make righteousness and unrighteousness the same, or the one a modification of the other, are failures. We recognize also that unrighteousness brings penalty. It is so in society, although society may set up a very untrue standard of right and wrong, artificial, not according to the standard which God has set up in our consciences and in the Christ. Yea, material rewards may come to men who are persistently acting on principles of unrighteousness, acting selfishly, i. e. in an ungodly manner. Very often it is so. This brings in confusion of mind. It creates perplexity. So much so that many men are led by it to the illegitimate inference, that verily there is no special reward for the righteous, verily there is no God that judgeth in the Earth. And as *material* rewards are the only ones that men of perverted minds and corrupted feelings appreciate, the acting so as to get these material rewards is common. Not only do industry and faithfulness bring these material rewards, but oftentimes dishonesty, shrewdness, heartlessness in bargaining and in taking advantage of men, bring them. Gambling brings them; gambling in many forms. Herein is the source of one of the strongest and most universal temptations of our life. A man does not seem any the worse, so far as the outside appearances of his life are concerned, because of transactions that are not honorable and honest. Oftentimes he seems better; he has acquired wealth and seems to have acquired importance.

And this fact alone ought to be enough to assure us that material rewards are not the only or the chief rewards which God gives. Man looks at the outward appearance, God looks at the heart, at that which is inward. Intellectual shrewdness and unscrupulousness often bring gold to the coffers, but they never bring sensitiveness to the conscience, nor purity into the feeling, nor piety into the heart. Much otherwise. The man who has educated himself into that state in which he has ceased to be a tender-hearted, humane, brotherly man, and has sunk into a mere trafficker, to whom there is only one hell, to be poor, and only one heaven, to be rich, that man is not to be admired. If you have any feeling to expend on him, let it be pity, although even that will by no means be appreciated. If we are to understand anything about Retribution, about the law of rewards and punishments, we must look deeper than the outside, into the heart and intellect and conscience, the inward condition.

Righteousness and unrighteousness, happiness and misery, are not expressible in terms of material gifts. The kingdom of God is within you.

saith the Lord; so is the kingdom of the Devil.

Thus, it is evident that in considering this theme of Retribution, we have to look below the surface. We have to school ourselves into the recognition that a man is rich or poor *really* not according to what he *has* but according to what he *is*.

Every one knows how vigorous, of late years, has been the assault upon the idea of a material hell. And many there be who seem to have explored the Universe and have not found it. If they would explore some of the courts and alleys of our great cities, if they would go into some of the dens and dungeons which, to thousands of people, supply the only place they can call home, if they would acquaint themselves with the horrors of society in some of their most terrific, loathsome and appalling forms, it would surely dawn upon them that there was a use even yet for the word "hell," even in its material expression. I am quite ready to admit that nowhere in the Universe can you find *God's Hell*, but you can find that which man has made. I hope that none of us may ever find that which was prepared for the devil and his angels. Men have been determined, I know, to make the idea of hell ridiculous. Granted that the materialism is only imagery, taken from the refuse heaps and the purifying fires which consumed the putrefying carcases of the Judean valleys, yet imagery has something behind it which it bodies forth. The whole material world is, I apprehend, but a parable of the spiritual world.

You know how valorously men have contended against the continuousness of the punishment of sin, but every man who sees below the surface of things must recognize that a man can sooner be divorced from his shadow than punishment can be separated from sin. Sin is self-willed separation from God, unrepentant lawlessness of soul, and as long as sin continues the punishment which is inherent in it, the punishment which comes from the indwelling opposition of the soul to God, whatever it be, must continue. The proof that one form of the presentation of a fact cannot be the true one, is no argument that all presentations of it are untrue. No one has ever yet discovered a way to make a hardened, unrepenting man righteous or happy, so long as he continues in that condition.

No one has ever yet discovered a method to prevent the working of the law, "whatsoever a man soweth that shall he also reap." No man has ever discovered where there is an element of injustice in the principle on which judgment turns, that a man should receive the deeds done in the body according to that he had done, whether it be good or bad.

Nor has any one discovered a way whereby a

man shall still be a man and yet be deprived of his power of choice, so as to be made righteous against his own will or wish. While it is altogether unbecoming of us to dogmatize on the only partially revealed future, yet we must not shrink from utterance of truth and fact as revealed *in* us, in the recognized laws of our nature, especially when they are clearly corroborated by the teachings of Scripture. The soul needs medicine as well as food.

I am not competent fully to expound all our Lord's words on retribution. As far as my own preferences are concerned, I should rather always quote them in their literalness and let them stand unmodified and unaltered by anything I might say. Thus the man who has any objection to urge, would have his controversy transferred from the servant to the master.

That there is, on the part of some of us, preachers and hearers, much of disgraceful trifling with these utterances on retribution, and on behalf of others much equally disgraceful dogmatism, I cannot omit to notice. But there are some facts which we cannot but recognize, unless we wilfully blind ourselves to their existence, such facts as that everywhere sin brings some kind of misery, misery physical and misery mental. This and other like facts are as patent as the noon-day. We recognize that there is a destructive power in this world, steadily and persistently working. Oftentimes men seem madly bent on their own destruction. Nothing stops them, nothing arrests them. Judgment seems to be lost and reason to be dethroned. All badness has an accompanying madness concealed in it. It would seem as though mankind was preyed upon by some power outside itself, bent on destroying it. Apart from all Scripture revelation, that would be the conclusion at which serious students of the problem would arrive. We shrink from acknowledging an invisible Satanic personal power, operative upon the spirit of man, and yet nothing short of this can account for that terrible tendency to self-destruction, which we find in our race. The New Testament acknowledges this power. It represents its concentrated malignity as focussing itself to destroy this Jesus Christ of ours. Our Lord says of it, 'it is able to destroy both soul and body in hell' and He tells us to fear it. It is revealed that Jesus the Christ came to destroy the works of the devil. There are some who jest at these ideas; but there cannot be any doubt of their existence on the New Testament page. That which our Lord has revealed, accounts for so much which we recognize in our human life that it seems to me to offer a solution of a very dark problem.

Perhaps some one is saying within himself,—what a terrible thing it is to be born exposed to such a power! It would be if it were an Omnipotent power, or a power which we could not resist, a power from which we could get no deliverance. But man is not left in this wretched and helpless state. The Deliverer is revealed; the One who comes between him and it to rescue all who put themselves under His protection. I cannot delay to remind you of that fact. At this point a question leaps into form — can the human lose its character as human and actually become devilish? The three stages of sinfulness as set forth by the Apostle, are these, 'earthly, sensual, devilish!' And we ourselves, in our common speech, recognize these three grades.

There are some things which men do which cannot properly be characterized as either 'earthly' or 'sensual'; we are driven to the use of the third term because neither of the others is felt to be accurate. When we consider such cases as I could name, such cases as will occur to you all, they compel us to face the question: "Is it possible that there can be such an inversion of human nature that good should always appear evil and evil good?" Is it possible for men to be permanently fixed in a spiritual condition in which malice, envy, and hate banish all possibility of love, esteem and affection? For myself I don't know; I cannot answer these questions. They have to be faced. Till they are answered, we cannot affirm, as of clear knowledge, the terminableness of sin or the terminableness of its inherent and inevitable punishment of itself beyond that point in life we call death. Every man who speaks on this theme should first pray God to give him humility and to take from him the cantankerous spirit of the controversialist. I am sincere when I say that I do not wish to speak as an opponent of any sectarian of any kind. If any brother man has had a revelation from God, either through Scripture, or independently of it, which has assured his mind that "not one life shall be destroyed, nor perish in the formless void, when God hath made the pile complete," he is of all men to be envied. No such revelation has come to my own mind from any source. While no one present can shrink from the unfeeling dogmatist on this question of the future of the man who calls evil good and good evil, more than I do, yet if I were to affirm that I had met with a full revelation of the final rescue of every soul of man from sin and its consequences, I should put on record in the most solemn act of my life a dreadful falsehood. This is not a matter of one man's opinion or another's; it is a matter of revelation.

I admit that it seems certain that all revelation on all themes which concern man and the possibilities of his nature, may not belong to this world, cannot belong to it. A fuller revelation doubtless will greet us on the other shore, for we have only the beginning of things here. The unfolding will go on forever and ever. This is only according to the laws we recognize as existing for our minds now. That condition of mind in which men demand that everything be revealed to them, here and now, about the future of all who constitute this human race, or they will have nothing to do with God and religion, seems, I should think, to us all, about as proud, tyrannical, wilful and unreasonable a state as any man can be in. There is really nothing to be done with a man in that condition, except to let him alone. Such a state is at the very antipodes of all teachableness. It is a compound of ignorance and wilfulness. A man says to me, 'I can't believe in a God who delights in damning men.' Nor can I. There is no such God revealed in the New Testament, from the lips of Jesus or his Apostles. "I have no pleasure in the death of the wicked, but rather that the wicked should turn and live." We damn ourselves, we damn one another, we unite with that Satanic power whose delight is rebellion against God. We worship the devil rather than God,— we do all this and thus destroy ourselves and our fellow-creatures, but the God revealed in Jesus Christ is in eternal antagonism to all this. There is no sin in God; God is light and in Him is no darkness at all; God is love, in him is no hate to you or me or anyone. That which is not in the Divine Nature can never come forth from it. Nothing is more simple and incontrovertible than that. We want clearly to understand, in these days, that there is ever a distinction to be made between the revelations which have come to us in Jesus Christ and the *inferences* which men have drawn from them. We must take good heed never to be so wedded to our own views and opinions, simply because they are ours, as not to be willing and ready to be led by the action of the Holy Spirit on our spirits into higher perceptions of truth. If we get into that state we shall be as a man who should put iron shutters up to every window in his house so that the sunlight should not interfere with his enjoyment of the light of his own candles. There is nothing more fatal to mental growth and to growth in grace, than proud, self-willed opinionativeness. The sincere mind is an open mind; the truthful mind is open — not a vacillating one — far from that. It holds what it has, but it reaches forth to that which is beyond. A man without principles and convictions is the prey of the next evil man or evil spirit that assaults him. God has more light and truth to break forth from His Holy Word, but from that Holy Word, Jesus Christ has broken forth this light and this truth already, that union with Him is life, separation from Him is death, whatever be included in that word. It will be proved yet to demonstration that whoever is of the truth heareth Christ's voice; that no true man ever yet took sides against God's Christ when that Christ was fully and fairly presented to his heart and understanding. And this also I believe will be shown, that there has never been any decree of God's which has condemned men to sin and suffer.

The sin and suffering are our own, the rescue and deliverance are God's. Separated from Him in whom the father of our spirits is revealed, we become a prey to evil spirits in the flesh and evil spirits out of the flesh. Not to be afraid of sin and sinners, and the arch-sinner of all we call Satan and the Devil, and to be afraid of God, the God revealed in Jesus Christ, this of all things betokens the extent of our removal from the original righteousness. What can be more frightful to a human soul than the loss of God? The word Atheism itself is a bottomless pit. "I will not leave you orphans," said our Lord to his disciples; fatherless ones. Oh no, He would not leave us in doubt that over us at all times, and in us by the gift of His spirit at all times was a Father, the Father of such a Son, the Father of Jesus Christ; is not that enough? What more dreadful mission is conceivable for a lost soul than to go about the world to try to rob other souls of their hope in a Father in heaven? Who of us would not prefer annihilation to this dreadful mission? And yet no man would or could believe it, but he who had so sinned himself into wretchedness as to *want* to believe it. And even he would doubt his own belief. Let us never lose sight of this fact that union with God in Christ is heaven, for the soul of man was made for that; separation from God in Christ is hell, the soul of man was never made for that. Whatever brings us nearer to God brings us into the sphere of ineffable reward, such as eye hath not seen, nor ear heard, neither hath entered into the heart of man to conceive; whatever separates us from Him brings us into that sphere of retribution into which we cannot look far, where the selfish and the loveless find those of their own order and kind. They *go* there, God does not send them; such is the revelation. There is no change in God, none in Christ. "He is the same yesterday, to-day and for ever." While I am persuaded that no man living is able fully to interpret the whole of this theme, yet I think we can say this much with confidence :—

1. That the Eternal One can make no compromise with sin. "If God were not sure to punish the evil, and to make it bear, so far as it remains evil, the weight of his condemnation, the good would lose for us its reality."

2. As to duration, that as long as the sin

lasts, so long will its appropriate punishment last.

3. That no punishment will be inflicted which will throw the Divine Character as revealed in Christ into discord with itself.

4. That, as there is no malice in the Divine nature and no cruelty, all punishment will have as its purpose an end worthy of the divine nature.

5. That future punishment will be to present sin as consequence to cause.

6. That it will be inevitable and not arbitrary.

7. That it will be of such a nature, that no enlightened mind in the Universe of God can offer any objection to it that shall not be unreasonable.

Ought I not to add for every perplexed soul on this and all other vital themes, " Come unto me all ye that labor and are heavy laden and ye shall find rest unto your souls."

VII.

MEANS AND END.

And why call ye me Lord, Lord, and do not the things which I say?—*Luke*, vi: 46.

ON February 20th, 1844, in the Supreme Court at Washington, a great speech was made by a man who must ever be allowed the *first* rank among the statesmen and orators of America. The speech is remarkable not alone for the purity of its English, not alone for the manliness of its style, for these remarks apply to all the speeches of this great man. It is noteworthy for the passionateness and evident genuineness of the sympathy which the speaker manifests with the truths and facts of the Christian religion, and with the means which are used and which are inevitable for its propagation.

A sum of money had been bequeathed to found a college in Philadelphia from within whose walls all Christian ministers were to be excluded. Daniel Webster argued that this exclusion virtually amounted to the ostracism of Christianity itself, and that it followed that in no true legal sense could this college take rank as a *charity*. The speech is memorable as embracing the views of the most statesmanlike mind, the most robust nature, this country has ever produced, on this one point, *the relation* of the *means to the end*, and the inevitable inference that must be drawn in regard to their judgment of the value of the end by those who neglect the means employed for the accomplishment of it. The *end* in view is the diffusion of Christianity among the people. The *means* used are; 1, the establishment by our Lord himself of the Ministry; 2, the bringing into existence of the Church; 3, the compilation of the Scriptures; 4, the ordinance of the Sabbath. This statesman, jurist, orator, this man of the first rank in each department, contends that so long as we treat the means that are inevitable for the diffusion of Christianity with contempt, it is vain and frivolous to be talking of any respect we may have for Christianity itself. Our actions give the lie to our words.

"There is a positive rejection of Christianity; because it rejects the ordinary means and agencies of Christianity. He who rejects the ordinary means of accomplishing an end means to defeat that end itself, or else he has no meaning. And this is true, although the means originally be means of human appointment, and not attaching to or resting on any higher authority."

Webster contends that there is nothing in the New Testament more clearly established by the Author of Christianity than the appointment of a Christian ministry. He asks, "Did a man ever live that had a respect for the Christian religion and yet had no regard for any one of its ministers?"

He contends further that religion is "the only solid basis of morals," and that moral instruction not resting on this basis is only a building upon sand. He contends that the moral law of the ten commandments includes the whole ten in its idea of morality. He suggests that the man who moves away the foundation of morals is aiming at the destruction of morality as well as Christianity. He further contends that Christianity is of such a nature that it belongs as really to children as to adults, and that there is neither religion, nor morals, nor reason in any course of action which sets aside the means that have been verified as necessary to the diffusion of that truth which is included in the word 'Christianity.'

He further remarks that "the observance of the Christian Sabbath is a part of Christianty in all its forms;" that "where there is no observance of the Christian Sabbath there will be no public worship of God," and he quotes with cordial approval and hearty endorsement an address which had just been delivered, in which are these words:—" you might as well put out the sun and think to enlighten the world with tapers, destroy the attraction of gravity and think to wield the Universe by human powers, as to extinguish the moral illumination of the Sabbath and break this glorious main-spring of the moral government of God." And when, with his strong manly eloquence, and his clear great intellect, he has examined the argument brought on the other side for allowing Girard College to be accepted as a charity, although from six years old to eighteen the youth there are to have no religious instruction, the orator seems to grow impatient with himself at the development of his argument, and lets himself out in one passionate sentence as he realizes what is involved in depriving these youths of their rights, and adds: "Why Sir, it is vain to talk about the destructive tendency of such a system; to argue upon it is to insult the understanding of every man; it is mere, sheer, low, ribald, vulgar deism, and infidelity."

Now I have made this copious reference to one of the most powerful orations that ever Webster made, because it contains the deliberate judgment of the greatest New Englander, the one who will be remembered and read and quoted, in the generations to come, oftener than any other, that I may have the best backing I can get for the enforcement upon your attention of the principle, that he who neglects the means conspires to defeat the end. One of the most unpromising features of our time is the seeming inability of so many people to perceive this very thing, the connection of means and end. Neglect the means and you are doing your best to defeat the end. I will not venture upon giving my opinion as to the causes of the condition in which so many find themselves, of having a sort of decent respect for some indefinite type of Christianity and yet to them Christianity is not necessary to morality, not necessary to good government, not necessary to citizenship, not necessary to personal development, not necessary to character, not necessary to anything. On its practical side, Christianity is bound up with the Sabbath, with the Church, with the Scriptures, with the Ministry of the Gospel. Through these, it gets voice, body and form. Without them it is a disembodied spirit. These are to it, what the lungs and limbs and nerves and veins and arteries are to the body. In this material world the spirit in man operates through these. There is no influence of the Spirit in man on this present order of things apart from these.

I am aware that there are very many persons over whom the irresistible reasoning of this most Titanic of Americans whom I have quoted, would have no influence. They have listened to tell-tale

Rumor which is always busy, and have heard this and that about him which, if true, indicates that he was by no means a perfect man. This is not a lecture on Webster. This is not the time nor the place to search into these reports. But this I will say, that I am ashamed for our intelligence; I am ashamed for our honesty; I am ashamed for our candor, I am ashamed for our Christianity, if we can allow a few beldame stories, such as are invented against all great men, to obscure our vision as to the real greatness of mind and heart, which dwelt in that imposing form.

The fruit of a choice apple tree is none the less luscious because for one month of the Spring time the canker-worm disfigured many of the leaves. I wish that with as much of truth we could all say as he said:—

"I thank God, that if I am gifted with little of that spirit which is able to raise mortals to the skies, I have yet none, as I trust, of that other spirit which would drag angels down."

It is no answer to the principle here asserted by this great man, the principle that the man who neglects the *means* aims to defeat the *end*, that sometimes the orator was not himself quite correct in his conduct. Who is? Which of us can stand up in that presence which searches the heart, and say that we have always been correct in our conduct? But does that make Christianity untrue?

Nay, it verifies its truth, when it says 'that there is not a just man upon earth that doeth good and sinneth not.' The inconsistencies of Christians have nothing to do with the truth of Christianity, or rather Christianity has nothing to do with them. It is not accountable for them. If we are to wait for perfect specimens of Christianity before there is any utterance of it, or any teaching of it, total silence must forever reign. Some knowledge is necessary to utterance but not perfect knowledge. Some experience of Christianity is necessary to the appreciation of its greatness, its grandeur, its benevolence, but not perfection of experience. Our preaching of it may often be, as Sheridan once remarked, "a poulterer's description of a phœnix," still any preaching of Christ and Him crucified is better than none, as St. Paul suggested when some were vile enough to preach Christ out of envy and strife, only to cause the Apostle pain, "Notwithstanding, whether in pretence or in truth, Christ is preached, and therein will I rejoice."

I wish that in these days Webster's great speech could be printed as a religious tract to be distributed broad-cast among people who credit themselves with intelligence. Do we not need it? Are there not many who assume that they are, in some sort of way, and in some sense of the word 'Christians' and yet who do not study the Scriptures, and do not use the means of grace, and have no reverence for the Sabbath, and seldom put themselves under the influence of any ministry of the Gospel? Such persons would feel aggrieved if it were said to them that they were seeking to defeat those ends which to Jesus Christ were so momentous that he held not himself back from agony and death that He might accomplish them. Yet, if these arguments of this greatest of Americans are unanswerable, it is true. No man is promoting the ends which our Lord came to accomplish, who is neglecting the Church, the Scriptures, the Ministry or the Sabbath. I wish to be reasonable. I would not press a man so hard as to create antagonism in his mind towards the truth. But, I think that none of you, I *hope* that none of you, would care to listen to any Minister who does not regard his allegiance to Christ as the first thing. There is no man whom I should myself more despise than he who standing in a Christian pulpit would say the thing which would make him popular, regardless of whether he believed it to be true or not. We have been hearing of late very much about the Old and the New. For myself I am not interested, as to whether a thing be old or new, I want to know if it be *true*. Is it in accord with the mind of Christ and the will of God? And this principle which the foremost statesman of New England has brought into the happiest form of expression, appears to me to be true. In neglecting the means we are aiming to defeat the end. Men who are not intelligently observing the Sabbath, elevating it in its uses above other days, are co-operating to defeat the ends for which the Sabbath was ordained. In not systematically and diligently using the means of grace, we are co-operating to defeat the end for which the means of grace were ordained — the spiritualization of the character. If we are at heart Christians and are not confessedly of the Church, we are silently (perhaps unintentionally and unconsciously), but really, aiming to defeat the end for which the Church of Christ was called into existence. What is lawful for one Christian must surely be lawful for all. Anyway, there must be something very special in the case of a Christian heart to justify its position of aloofness from a Christian church. I know that all Christian churches, in their administration, partake of human infirmitiy. But wherever there is the simple acknowledgment of Christ as supreme, the presence of human infirmity is reduced to a minimum of influence. There is however a blessing special to the church, a blessing of God which belongs to his disciples, and can belong in the nature of things to none other. Obedience always brings blessedness.

Is it not so in Nature? The mariner never thinks of entering into conflict with the laws of nature; he *conforms* to them, he obeys them. There is a blessing in obedience. There is destruction in disobedience. And so on land as on sea;—the farmer's prosperity depends upon his understanding the laws of vegetable and animal life and co-operating with those laws. There is a blessing in *obedience* which can be obtained in no other way. It is so everywhere; in regard to our own personality; in regard to mental health and bodily health. Obey sanitary laws and you get the blessing, disobey them and you miss it. Now, it would be a strange inconsistency, if the Almighty should teach us of the way of obtaining a blessing in Nature, and contradict that truth in the highest region of all. Would it not be astonishing if obedience to material laws brought blessing, and disobedience to spiritual laws did not bring the opposite of blessing? If our Lord says to us, *Do so and so*, rely upon it that there is some benevolent reason why we should do it. All Divine commands are founded in benevolence. All Divine institutions are founded in benevolence. That is true of the Church; it is true of the Sabbath; it is true of the Scriptures; it is true of the Ministry; of all these four things to which Webster referred as means to the end of diffusing Christianity. No man of you is more sensitive than I am to the unchristian elements which have been introduced by fallen and fallible men into church life. So oppressive have they been at times to my spirit, so hateful have they seemed, so hot has been my aversion to them, that I have had fight after fight with myself to keep in the Ministry. I believe in Christianity with all my intellect and with all my heart. Nothing is so dear to me as Christian truth. It grows upon me all the time. The more I look into the New Testament the more I believe in its inspiration. It is incalculably nobler in its temper, immeasurably higher in its spirituality than anything I find elsewhere. Men wrote it, but it is free from the weaknesses, the meannesses, the jealousies, the sectarianisms of men. God ruled while men wrote, that is what I mean by inspiration. God's mind dominated man's. God's mind was uppermost and man's undermost. God's thought dominated man's opinion and held it in subjection. The men who wrote were so full of God that they could do no other than write his thoughts. It is like as when a lawyer has been living day and night in Blackstone. He becomes so dominated by him that his own thought is permeated by Blackstone. Or, as when a surgeon has been submitting himself to the influence and teaching of Sir Astley Cooper, he is controlled by him. These men were what Schleirmacher would call, " God-intoxicated men." They were filled full of Christ and so spake the Divine thought. They could do no other. They spake as seeing Him who is invisible, and they acted as seeing him who is invisible. And so, you have only to take any volume of Divinity written by man, any church articles formulated by man, and compare them with the spirit and temper of the Scriptures to see the incomparableness of the Scriptures. They are for all time, and not for any single age.

And here in these Scriptures we find Christ's idea of the Church, and the Apostolic idea. We do not realize them. The Scripture idea of the Church is entirely free from all such divisions as we have in denominationalism. The Church of the New Testament is the fraternity of all who love and serve Christ. If a man will not submit his will and spirit to Christ, he does not belong to the Church, if he does submit his will and spirit to Christ he belongs to the church. But, in Scripture, faith always means character, internal character, the internal character which recognizes Jesus when it sees Him and clings to Him. It is nothing less than a perversion of Scripture to identify faith with opinion. Now, while we are living below the Scripture idea of the church of Christ, yet we are aiming at it and trying to realize it, and under this constant aim, the Church will grow more and more Christlike in its spirit. And it is the duty of all who are Christian in hope and in heart to unite with it openly and unabashed.

Why call ye me Lord, Lord and do not the thing which I say? Church membership is not a matter of personal perfection or imperfection. It is a matter of obedience to the Lord Jesus Christ. I am obliged to put it on that simple ground. I should not be truthful to my own convictions if I put it on any other. It is a means of grace, if we use the means, we are manifestly aiming at the end.

And then again as to the Sabbath — another means for the diffusion of Christianity. It is founded in benevolence. I could not believe in a God who made it necessary for five-sixths of this human race to earn their bread by the sweat of the brow, or the sweat of the brain, if he let them work on and on without any authoritative command periodically to stop. That would indicate him a slave-master, not a God. Three-hundred and sixty-five days in every year devoted to unbroken toil, who could believe that such a command ever came from a good God? Not that I believe that hand work is in these days of ours the most exhausting work. No! — brain-work, continued on and on, is the wear and tear of life. The brain-workers more than the hand-workers need to stop every seventh day, and shut down business and bolt and bar the door on it, and turn their attention to something entirely different. For relief comes to the brain, not from total cessation of thinking, that is impossible, but from *other* thinking. And the more entirely different the theme the more recuperative it is. That is the reason why some of our greatest English statesmen, yes and our greatest American lawyers, have been among the healthiest and strongest minds. Gladstone can sit and listen to a sermon with as much enjoyment of it as though it was a revelation to him. A late Lord Chancellor, who presided over the House of Peers, taught a Sunday School class. The great pleader at the American bar, Choate, could continuously and untiringly enjoy the simple evangelical ministry of Dr. Adams. Webster was a constant attendant on worship. These men used the means as seeing that the only way to accomplish the end was to use them. How is it possible to believe that any one sees the momentousness of Christianity and its relation to our life here and hereafter if he neglect the means appointed for its propagation? Even Charity, hard as she may try, cannot believe it. To every such person the question comes direct from the lips of Jesus.—"Why call ye me Lord, Lord, and do not the things which I say?"

VIII.

"WORSHIP GOD."

> Then saith he unto me, See thou do it not: for I am thy fellow-servant, and of thy brethren the prophets, and of them which keep the sayings of this book: worship God.— *Revelations*, xxii: 9.

IT may seem strange to some of you that I should introduce such a simple theme as this to a congregation assembled for the avowed purpose of worshipping God. I do not wish to insult your intelligence; very far from that. I have always tried to give all proper deference and respect to intelligence, believing, as I do, that true and real Christian preaching is certain to deepen, broaden, elevate and ennoble the intelligence of those who submit themselves to it. Why not? Is it not occupied with the profoundest of all themes? What theme can be profounder than the nature of God, the nature of man, and the relation of man to God? If there be any theme profounder than that I would like to know what it is. And should there be anyone here inclined to say that we can know nothing about it, or next to nothing, or only a very little, I beg to join issue with that individual. He is not speaking intelligently, not speaking out of his own individuality, only reiterating phrases which he has learnt from others. Supposing I never see the artist who painted that interesting animal picture "Dignity and Impudence." I have never looked on his face, never talked with him, never asked him as to his likes and dislikes. But I look on his picture, study it, not its coloring only or chiefly, or its drawing, but its expressiveness.

And as I look and look I say to myself—Landseer evidently had a wonderful fondness for dogs. He must have had it, or he could not have put that expression into the faces of those dogs. Those eyes are almost human in their expressiveness. And so, take any work of any man, and study it, and you will learn something about the man. Not everything, by any means, but something. If however in addition to that picture you had studied other pictures of Landseer, your knowledge of the man would have grown more and more; if then you had talked with people who had visited him, held social converse with him, walked with him, ate with him, been with him in trouble and joy, your knowledge would have grown into a kind of intimacy, and yet you have never seen the man. But without seeing him, you have true knowledge of him. And so it is in respect to every one. So it is in respect to God Himself. You can know much of Him. All his works speak of Him. There is strength in Him says the mighty mountain. There is majesty in Him say the Niagaras as they roar. There is light in Him, says the sun. There is order in Him say the stars; such order, says the comet, such punctuality in fulfilling His appointments, that I will be back again from my measureless orbit to a second. There is love in Him says Jesus Christ. And Jesus Christ is as much a fact as is this American Nation. We can know enough about God to occupy us for the years we have here. Yea: we can know more about Him than these few years can ever exhaust.

Of course no one knows a thing, much less a person with any respectable degree of knowledge, who does not come into some kind of personal relationship with the thing or person. Our relationship to God must be personal. It must be something more than organic. The beasts that roam the forests, the cattle on a thousand hills, have some sort of relationship to God. He provides for them. He must delight in them. The song of the bird, the mild content of the domesticated cow, the proud beauty of the Arab steed, the majesty of the lion, these must delight Him. They express some thought and feeling in the Divine mind, very imperfectly, very blunderingly, very distantly, but still enough to start us thinking and inquiring. And is not that an excellent use? Is it not much to be preferred that a man should be perplexed with mysteries than that he should be uninterested in anything, torpid and indifferent to a most shameful degree? It is even to be preferred that a man should pass along the way of life grumbling at everything he meets than that he should not exist at all, although you and I perhaps do not want to meet that man too often. But still, God has some use for him, as He has for a mosquito, although I have never discovered what it is. Do you suppose that the Almighty has to give an account of everything he does and makes to you and me? I believe that the mysteries of life have a use and service in regard to man which is by no means despicable. The fact that there is so much unknown makes life doubly interesting. I am persuaded that one reason why this country is at the present day perhaps the most interesting country on the face of the earth lies in the fact of its being only partially developed, and in the other fact that we are trying experiments all the while, the great experiment of making all nations into one nation. And the very fact that our politicians and others make such emphatic assertions as to our greatness and our excellency is a sign that we are a little bit afraid as to where the experiment will land us, and those who are to come after us. There is this consolation, however, that we cannot with our democracy do very much worse than others have done with their monarchies and aristocracies, but if we do not do better, and very much better, a heavy cloud of disappointment will hang over the whole earth for ages to come. Perhaps some are inclined to say, " Well, we shall know nothing about it; we shall be away from here." Don't be so sure, my friend. If Moses and Elijah knew what was being transacted on this earth after they had left it, and came to that Mount of Transfiguration, we have more than a suggestion that we are to know about this earth after we have left it. The putting off this prison-house of a material body is not going to produce total separation between this earth and our future, unless all the hints of Scripture are misleading. The doctrine of the solidarity of the human race — that what affects one affects all — is full of meaning. There is more in Scripture than any of you suppose upon the connection of the eternal future with the present, and the carrying of the present into the future, But I will not be tempted along that line now.

We know enough of God to enable us to worship Him and serve Him. That is the practical thing. What is worship? Admiration leading to imitation. Nothing short of that. That is our

Lord's idea of it as you will find in the Sermon on the Mount. In Wordsworth's poems there are some excellent hints on this subject, which I cannot quote. So also in Tennyson. So also in Longfellow. These men will all help you to get into that state of mind in which you are capable of worship. For not all men are capable of such admiration as will lead to imitation. God made man capable originally. This state of admiration leading to imitation was the easy, natural state of the first man. That is the Mosaic idea. But our fathers fell out from that ability, and we have fallen out still more, till men and women have lost this ability of admiration to the point of imitation. There are many things in the writings of Thomas Carlyle which none of us can accept. But there is one feature in the rugged old man which I have always appreciated, his intense admiration for his heroes, Cromwell, Frederick the Great, Knox, Mahomet, and others. He delights in their power and ability, and in their love of righteousness. If only we could search sufficiently into character to verify the remark, I think we should find that no man was ever really good or really great who had not in him a strong tendency to idolize somebody. For what does this tendency mean? It means that in the individual there is great *receptive* power, great *heart* power, great *love* power. And what does that mean, but great power of goodness? A man's judgment may be at fault and he may choose an unworthy object, but there will be something in his object that fascinates and holds him. A man who has the capacity of great admiration has not and cannot have the ability of great enviousness of disposition. For the two traits are psychologically incompatible. The one excludes the other.

We may laugh at Carlyle's hero-worship, but was it not much better than no ability of worship at all? *There* is the terrible defect, no ability of worship at all, indicating, as it does, low intellectualism, low heart power, low imaginativeness, low ideality, general inferiority all through. The ability of admiration must be in us, and it must be in us to the degree of imitation, or Jesus Christ Himself will have no power to fascinate and hold us. And if even the heroic character of Jesus, the masculine character of Jesus, the feminine character of Jesus, the superlatively human character of Jesus, the Divine character of Jesus, if *that* have no power to win us, and hold us, and draw us out, and bring us to our knees in worship, then, I know not what to say. Something terrible is the matter with that man's nature which does not respond to the ineffable excellency which is in Christ Jesus our Lord. It is of no use deceiving men. That is cruel. I say, wherever there is no response to the fully presented character of Jesus Christ, wherever it does not win admiration, leading to imitation, in a word worship, there is something seriously wrong in that nature. St. Paul, one of the most gifted men of the world, one of the most considerate, one of the most loving and humane, even he could not refrain himself when he thought of Christ Jesus rejected, and said, "If any man love not the Lord Jesus Christ, let him be *anathema.*"

I admit that it does seem as though *every* nature ought to have in it this ability of worship. We see it to a most pitiful extent in many heathen people, giving up for the sake of their false deities so very, very much; so very much more than we give up for the sake of our Christ. And I think God Almighty respects and loves them and will not be hard upon them, probably put many of them into higher service in the hereafter than you and I shall reach. But the lesson we ought to learn from these heathen people is, that *theology* is not to be despised, that men will be this or that in life and feeling according to their theology, that to get a true theology is, after all, worth while. Doubtless there are people who assume that the theologic disputations of all ages are frivolous. But, let us not be in a hurry to concur in that opinion. If it be true that men will be this or that according to their ideas of what God is and what He requires of them, is it not worth while to be very careful lest we should get wrong views and opinions as to the nature of Diety? If I believe that the Almighty is simply Almighty, that that is His chief attribute, the result will be *fear*. My soul will crouch in His presence. I shall be but a slave. I cannot rise any higher than that. If on the other hand I believe that Deity has as its chief attribute easy good nature, no indignation in it, no hostility to anything; then I shall be sure to infer that good and evil are only names, words only, not things, And righteousness of thought and feeling will be impossible to me. The idea will help on the corruptness of my nature. It was so in Greece and Rome; their ideas of Deity were so corrupt that they corrupted the people. So long as Mars was worshipped as a Deity, war was perpetual. So long as Venus was a goddess, lust was inevitable. So long as the gods were treacherous the people were treacherous also. When religion's self is of such a nature that it corrupts the people, the decline and fall are very rapid. And so, it would seem that the disputations of theologians are not meaningless or useless. They are vital. To get at the truth is worth in its result all that we can sacrifice of ease and peace. If we do not care what the truth is, then, well then — God help us — that is all I can say.

Recognizing this ability of worship as being in

our constitution, a part of our manhood, that which lifts us above the animal, that which bespeaks us of a higher order of being; and stating it, as we have done in this formula, 'admiration leading to imitation'—does it not appear that whatever we admire to the point of imitation we worship? Please to be careful in taking into your memory the whole of this phrase, admiration to the point of imitation. There may be admiration of so feeble a kind that it does not produce any desire to imitate. There may be imitation which does not involve admiration. It is mere slavishness and weakness, the inability to be even amiably individual. The extent to which the thing which is temporarily fashionable in dress or anything else is adopted shows how slavish and how weak we all are. Imitation there may be without admiration, admiration without imitation, but when we get admiration up to the point of imitation then we have worship.

And this worshipfulness in us may produce very disastrous results to character when the object is unworthy. We have read of devil worship. Of course we assume that in an advanced civilization like our own, we are leagues away from this. I wish with all my heart that I could believe it. Scripture reveals to us an Evil Personality which it calls the Prince of Darkness. It tells us that He is the Father of Lies, the Accuser of the

Brethren, the Devourer, the One who offers to men (as he did to Jesus) power and wealth if only they will take it in his way, if only they will fall down and worship Him. He is represented as being the enslaver of the human soul, as being the arch-enemy of Christ, as great in wiles and snares, as inciting to sin, as serpentine in his nature, as not only at one time a roaring lion, but at another as a snake in the grass, the arch-traitor, the arch-deceiver. This is the New Testament revelation of the character of this Prince of Darkness. You say you don't believe in him. I hope not. But some do, for they imitate him. They admire his methods and adopt them. If, you mean, that you don't believe in his existence, then you know more than Jesus Christ knows. About which I for one have an honest doubt. This Prince of Darkness has been very successful in this world. From the time of Adam he has been at work here, injecting into the minds of men wrong views about God, and about themselves. He cannot eradicate from the constitution of man the propensity to worship and so he says "worship me; I like to be worshiped. Admire my methods, imitate my way of action," (for that is worship.) Worship is not simply bending the knee. It is admiration to the point of imitation. And so it comes to this that if we adopt the methods which are not approved by Jesus the Christ but *are* approved by the Tempter of Jesus, we worship, I do not like to admit it, I shrink from the admission, but I cannot see any way of escape, we worship the devil. I am compelled to go a step farther yet and say that if our souls were so purified that evil would be a positive pain to us, as much of a pain to the soul as the stab of a poniard to the body, our perceptions would be so spiritualized that the extent to which devil worship prevails would appear to us frightful and horrible. That I may not seem to be making vain and vague general charges against an impersonal somebody about whom none of you are concerned, let me ask you to recall some of the acknowledged facts of common life. This evil one against whom our Lord warns us is called "The Father of Lies." Think how many people there are who do not shrink from falsehood when there is anything to be gained by it. Whom do these worship? Whom do they imitate?

This Evil Personality is called, "The Accuser of the Brethren." Are there no persons living in the world who seem to take a malicious and cruel delight in insinuations which undermine the character of others—specially of Christian men and women? Whom do these worship? They who systematically betray others and deceive others, who lay traps for them and snares for them—whom do these worship? They worship Him whom they imitate; there is no other answer. We really need not take ship and cross the seas to find devil-worship. Unless the teaching of Jesus is not reliable, it is nearer home than that.

But I must turn away from it;—it is too painful a theme to dwell on for more than a moment. Jesus the Christ by the gift of the Holy Spirit can *deliver* us from this frightful worship, but no one else can. It is His mission on this earth, to deliver us from it. Let us learn more and more to admire and imitate Him that we may overcome it. For the full consequences of it are not seen here on earth. The end is not by and by.

My time is passing, but it would not do to stop at this point. I must detain you a minute or two longer while I say that there is nothing that you and I need for our enlightenment and enlivenment so much as a more simple and earnest worship of God. Our minds grow languid, our intellect becomes torpid, our affections loose their youthful freshness and energy if we do not keep before us some one to admire and imitate, some one to worship. Practically, to us, God is Jesus Christ. We cannot get above what He has revealed. If you think otherwise try it. In the Church we need a more simple, hearty, *enthusiastic* worship of God. I hope you will not be frightened at that word 'enthusiastic.' It does not mean *fanatic*. Fanaticism is blind emotion, uncurbed by reason, unchecked by intellect. It is the steam in the engine uncontrolled by the hand of the engineer. But enthusiasm—it means the Spirit of God in the intellect, the Spirit of God in the reason, the Spirit of God in the heart and so in the whole personality and in the whole life. I was telling some friends the other night about a clergyman in London, sitting in the retiring room of a Cemetery Chapel, waiting patiently for a funeral which was much behind the appointed time, when suddenly the sexton opened the door, and said to the clergyman, "If you please, Sir, the Corpse's brother wants to speak with you." The astonished clergyman was for a moment appalled at the idea of meeting a Corpse's brother, hardly knowing whether it would be a live or dead man. I have sometimes thought that some of our churches might not inaptly be designated as a Corpse's brother. I have no ambition to be tied to any such church. If there be any place where the smell of death is not only unpleasant but repulsive, it is in a church whose very foundation is life from the dead. As one has said, "Our churches as mere organized bodies are comely enough, and they are not without some degree of life and strength. They work easily, quietly, philosophically, and cautiously, like a man of seventy years of age who is careful in all his movements, and afraid of doing too much. But you must excuse me when I say that we are wanting in the strength and vigor and energy of a man of twenty-five. We are old before our time."

We need to *worship God*. That is all. Everything we need would come if only we could *worship*. The coldness would leave the region of the heart. There would come more *thinking* power into the intellect. The glories of the Apocalypse would not be too glorious for the regenerated imagination. Much of the Scripture which is now dark to us, because out of the reach of our experience, would become clear. Our horizon would stretch out and out beyond the present limits of vision. How often it is with us as with those painters who paint a beautiful little bit of country all shut in with rocks and hills, not even a glimpse of luminous sky above to speak of something else than this ornate little prison. The *greatest* painters never do that. They leave an outlook. They suggest infinite distances. Our life, the life of every Unchristianized man is shut in. It has no outlook. What would the New Testament be without the Book of the Revelation of St. John? That gives it artistic completeness. The end of the Book of Revelation is, "The end of the great tragedy of life. The beast has vanished; the hissing of the unclean spirits has been silenced; the Dragon, the old serpent called the Devil and Satan, is bound; the tempest has ceased; the thunders are hushed; the smoke and the clouds are swept away; the light shines, and the pinnacles of the New Jerusalem come forth to view. Life is blessed in that city. There shall be no more curse, no more sorrow, no more crying, no more pain. God shall wipe away all tears from their eyes."

You call that poetry, do you? Suppose it is poetry, what then? No poet ever yet equalled the fact which he poetized, as no painter ever yet mixed colors equal to those in nature. When the poetry is gone out of our life, it is like the sappiness gone out of the tree; all that is left is sawdust. "Worship God" and the poetry will return into your dried-up lives, as the Psalmist suggests in the words, "Bless the Lord, O my soul, and all that is within me bless His holy name."

IX.

THE CHILD AND HIS DUES.

"Do not sin against the child."— *Genesis*, xlii : 22.

THESE words were spoken by the eldest born of Israel's sons when there was a conspiracy among them to deprive Joseph of his birthright in the family. There are so many aspects of the great theme of the Incarnation that one must necessarily feel no little perplexity when obliged to select the ideas to be presented on any special occasion. So much must be left unsaid. Our theme at the best must be wretchedly incomplete. The Incarnation is the miracle of miracles. It is too *subtle* a theme for the Intellect. When we try to satisfy the mind we come to a point beyond which we cannot pass by any intellectual process. And yet, this limitation ought not to produce any kind of scepticism as to the fact itself. For all life in its origin is mysterious. And if the facts about it were not so common, if men were not born into the world every day, we should doubtless perceive more readily than we do how very little indeed man's part is in the production of any thing. All vital facts elude us. They *are;* but we cannot tell *how* they are.

This we know, however, that intellect is not everything in us. Our nature comprises much else than the intellectual. There are facts for the heart of man which once apprehended never leave us. And this of the Incarnation is one. How shall Deity so reveal Himself to man as to win his confidence and love? That is the great practical question of religion. The answer to that question is the Incarnation — God manifest in the flesh. If we were inclined to look at this fact philosophically, it would be easy to show that in man's nature there is the inwrought expectation of an Incarnation. For what is idolatry but an attempt on man's part to bring God within human limitations? Jesus Christ satisfies that instinct in man which leads to idolatry. The instinct must be gratified. The Incarnation is the Divine answer to that instinct. Jesus coming into humanity becomes the heart of humanity. You cannot now put any one else than Jesus Christ at the centre of our life. In the Kingdom of Heaven, superiority of nature gives superiority of position. There is nothing arbitrary or forced in the supremacy of Jesus.

In the Incarnation, God joins himself to our humanity as never before, joins himself to our childhood as well as to our manhood. And the fact that I want to put above every other in this morning's meditation is this, that God can and does speak through childhood as well as through fully developed manhood. Childhood is no hindrance to the work of the Spirit of God, but a necessary stage in the work, a stage which if lost can never be fully recovered. And as I am sure that we have never given sufficient thought to the meaning of the impressibility of childhood, and have never enough apprehended that our great religious opportunity is in the first few years of a child's life,— I shall use the brief time allotted to me at this Christmas service in a presentation of such ideas as may help towards a revision of our creed on this point. When we look at the *babe* of Bethlehem, is not the thought irresistible, God can speak to us through the helplessness of the babe. And when we watch that babe as it is hurried away from persecution, and think that it is carried in the fostering arms of *motherhood*, can we resist the thought, that the preservation of the Kingdom of God in the earth is dependent on the sanctification and consecration of motherhood? The Incarnation is the elevation of motherhood to a place it had never had in any heathen or pagan country. The preservation of God's Kingdom in the world is dependent, so it seems, on the sanctification of those human instincts which the Creator has sown in our nature. Surely *that* is a great enough truth to justify the Kingdom of God being hidden away in the infanthood of a babe. The tendency of religion has often been to say, crucify your social instincts. They are unholy and unclean. Christianity says, consecrate them and they immediately become holy and clean. Christianity began with a consecrated childhood and a consecrated motherhood. Through these relationships God spake his first parental word in this dispensation in which we now live.

If you will allow me the expression — all the gentlenesses and delicacies, all the modesties and sweet refinements of the Kingdom of God, were brought into human expression in that babe and that mother. That child stood for all children, that mother for all mothers thenceforth. God spake through that child in order that we might learn that He could speak and did speak through childhood. Why should God limit himself to the conditions of a child's nature? Because there is a language to be spoken through the child which can never be spoken except through the child. Because there is a rebuke to be given to our proud grown-up intellectualism which arrogates to itself the prerogative of being God's voice and his only voice. And the reason why we have so often and so sorely missed the meaning of this childhood of Jesus as a part of the revelation of God is in this — that we have thought of religion as something intellectual, simply — a matter of doctrines and creeds, and logical propositions. And have we not asked what can a child know of the truth or falsity of these? A sufficient answer would be.—' It will know just what its father and mother tell it, for a child is so constituted that it believes in its father and mother.' But we will not give that answer. We go deeper than that, and first of all deny that religion consists in doctrines and creeds and intellectual propositions, any more than a dinner consists of the printed receipts of a Cookery Book. Religion is aback of these literary productions. It consists of love to God and love to man.

Love is not an intellectual thing at all. The essence of the Christian religion is love. That elevates it above every other religion the human race has ever known. Can a child love? Can it love father or mother? Can it depend on father and mother? Can it confide in father or mother? If so, it can love God. If so it can love man, for father and mother represent mankind to it. We who are adults love mankind to the extent (and only to the extent) to which we love the representatives of it whom we know.

Set God as He is in Jesus Christ before the heart of a child, and will there be no response in that heart? Then there has been something terribly atheistic in the secondary parenthood of that child. The primary parenthood is in God — the secondary parenthood in man. I go aback of secondary parenthood, aback of all ideas—opinions, creeds and formularies of man's devising, and I aver that it is absolutely impossible in the nature of things that Almighty God can so form the spirits he puts into human bodies as that in them from the first there shall be a negative of Himself. The root of the error is in this assumption, that a child's nature is animal and irreligious, an idea that never originated in Christianity but in paganism and gross materialism. A too narrow view of religion, and a too narrow view of childhood, have landed us in ideas and in practices which are most assuredly Anti-Christian. The view that religion is something to be learned from without and not something to be evolved from within, something intellectual, not affectional and vital, is at the root of this most serious error, an error so radical and serious that I verily believe that such themes as that recently discussed over the Andover professorship, are the veriest trifles in comparison with it. If religion be a mere intellectual acquirement like a knowledge of the history of philosophy, of course it would be useless to expect children to know anything about it, or to have any experience of it. But if religion has its seat in the heart and in the will, if it be far more affectional than intellectual, then wherever affection and will are operative, religion is alike capable of being brought into operation. If there be no affection and no will in a child there can be no religion, if there *be* affection and will there can be religion also. On this point there cannot be a doubt as to what is the Scripture position. The Book which contains such sentences as these " Out of the heart are the issues of life," " With the heart man believeth unto righteousness," " Whosoever receiveth one such little child in my name receiveth me, but whosoever shall be a stumbling block in the way of these little ones which believe in me, it were better for him that a millstone were hanged about his neck and he drowned in the midst of the sea," I say as to the position of that Book on this question there can be no doubt. Then, why has the other position been held by so many, that religion is an intellectual and mental acqurement for adults and not an affectional relation towards God on the part of everyone? There is but one answer, " we err, not knowing the Scriptures, nor the power of God." So long as any of us are under the blight of the error that in order to be in any degree religious, it is necessary to be capable of judging and weighing evidence *pro* and *con*, so long we shall feel justified in holding that a Christian church is a confederation of adult persons, or persons who have arrived, as we say, at years of discretion. But if once we went to the Bible and bathed our souls in its baptismal waters, saturated ourselves with its spirit, it would be impossible for us to take that position. Many things would stand in the way, many facts, many passages of Holy Scripture, but chiefest of all obstacles would be that which we think of to-day, the great fact of the Incarnation of our Lord and Savior Jesus Christ. The babe at Bethlehem is the Divine Word in its tenderest and gentlest expression.

Now, this mistake as to the seat of all true religion, that it is in the intellect and not in the heart, is by no means trivial. It must, of necessity, influence all our practical church life. If children have divine relations and rights Godward, and we do not recognize them, and in our ignorance defraud the children of them, their whole life is likely to be of a different color and tendency from what it would otherwise be. It is easy to see this. If we believe that religion has its seat in the affections and not in the intellect, we shall perceive that the religious education of the child begins as soon as its affectional nature is capable of receiving impressions. How soon is that? How soon does a child know enough to distinguish between its own mother and a stranger? The first years of a child's life are years of impressions and nothing else. The age of reflection has not come, nor will for some time. The *plastic* age is the first. Every day, every hour, every moment, impressions are being made on the affectional nature of the child, impressions which will last as long as that nature lasts. That being so, is it possible to over-estimate the value of those first years for the highest purposes of life?

I wish that it were a proper thing for me to reproduce in your hearing some of the glowing words of an American Divine not long since deceased, whose influence on the ministers of our English Churches has been greater than that of all other American divines put together. Speaking on this theme, to which I have been led this morning, he says—"I have no scales to measure quantities of effect in this matter of early training, but I may be allowed to express my solemn conviction, that more, as a general fact, is done, or lost by neglect of doing, on a child's immortality, in the first three years of his life, than in all his years of discipline afterwards." And again he says still more emphatically, "Let every Christian father and mother understand, when their child is three years old, that they have done more than half of all they will ever do for his character." It is very remarkable that the greatest of all Pre-Christian philosophers, Plato, held substantially the same view. And when He whose word to us is law, before whose utterances our opinions hide their diminished heads in the dust, when He said, "Suffer the *little* children to come unto me and forbid them not, for of *such* is the Kingdom of Heaven," was He not saying the same thing, only in a divine way, as this Plato of the American pulpit?

But, some one might ask, how is it possible to give religious instruction to a child of three years of age? Religious instruction can be but little, but it is always safe to postpone religious instruction when the child is in the constant presence of religious character. Religious or irreligious *impressions* are produced from the earliest times. And of these we are now speaking. They are the most important. Religious *instruction* is only a part of religious education. All education begins at the cradle and continues as long as life lasts. Connecting the two dispensations once again, the greatest mind of Pre-Christian times will help us as to this matter when he says, "The best way of training the young, is to train yourself; not to admonish them, but to be always carrying out your own principles in practice." And our modern theological Plato says: "In this charge and nurture of infant children, nothing is to be done by an artificial lecturing process. The defect of our character is not to be made up by the sanctity of our words; we must be all that we would have our children feel and receive. Thus, if a man were to be set before a mirror, with the feeling that the exact image of what he *is* for the day, is there to be produced and left as a permanent and fixed image forever, to what carefulness, what delicate sincerity of spirit would he be moved. And will he be less moved to the same, when that mirror is the soul of his child?"

Thus it comes to pass that though parents may withhold religious *instruction* from their children they cannot withhold religious education. For it goes on by a Divine law, over which we have no control. Whenever a stronger, a more fixed and determined nature comes into perpetual contact with a younger and more plastic nature, the latter is educated by the former. The former impresses itself upon it. Hence the importance of the associations which children form. Hence the solemn duty which is laid upon parents to discriminate between the influences to which they subject their children. The more plastic the child the nobler in the long run will be his life, but the more care is necessary in its beginnings. I know that there is the Unseen Spirit of God working on the spirit of the child all the time. That spirit is stirring the mind into thought and the heart into feeling. But God has decreed that the ordinance of parenthood shall be the most powerful in all this world. Richard Baxter, the author of the Saint's Rest, gave it as his judgment that "Family instruction and government are God's appointed means of conversion—public ordinances of edification."

That may be the law to which practically there are exceptions, but this we may say unhesitatingly, that never can the Church of God do its Divinely-appointed work till there is intelligent co-operation between it and the family. And this also, that nothing outside the family can ever be powerful enough to neutralize the influence of family life if it be irreligious or to thoroughly undo its influences if it be religious. It is not conceivable that any one should ever love a child as a parent loves it, and therefore it is not conceivable that parents should ever deliberately do anything whereby their children may be injured. But error and love may dwell together in the same heart; ignorance and love may dwell together. There may be no perception of the relation of religion to happiness, no perception of the relation of the Christ of God to the development of character.

Men and women of average goodness, who would do anything in the world they thought necessary for the *world-life* of their children, have not got their eyes open to perceive that happiness depends on the *within* more than on the *without*. They do not for a moment despise Jesus Christ and His work, but they assume that religion can be left to take care of itself. They do not see that the presentation of Christ to the soul awakes into life something which is otherwise dormant. The question whether there is anything in Christ to touch into feeling and hope and confidence, a child's heart, has not been seriously considered. How it is, I know not, but the fact remains that even christianized people do not see how studiously our Lord *identifies himself* with the cause of the little child, and the cause of the poor and unfortunate, and every true minister will do the same. Our clients are those who cannot speak for themselves — the little child that cannot speak what it feels, the little child with its innate ideas, ideas not originated by teaching, ideas which are emotions struggling within, which God has inwrought into the soul; and the poor who dare not speak out what they feel, who have so generally in the past ages of the world been robbed and wronged; Christ identified himself with these. Let us not forget that wherever there is religious feeling, there is religious life. This religious feeling in childhood is to be developed as the basis of religious action in manhood. It is in the soul of man as it was in the creation of this material world. First of all there was the chaos, the sweltering surging waters, and the spirit of God moving on the face of the waters.

But out of it came the Cosmos — the Divine order — the solid earth with its mineral wealth and its treasures of coal ready for the habitation of man; but the solidity followed the liquidity; and so it is with a human soul. At first there is religious feeling, out of which under proper culture and the o'erbrooding spirit of God, will grow the solid, indestructible convictions of manhood and womanhood. But, if you repress the feeling, and throw cold water on it when it glows in childhood, how are you to get your convictions in manhood? You have destroyed the material out of which convictions are made.

Before the animal passions begin to assert themselves, as in youth or early manhood, there should have been evolved in the soul a religious love which shall control and moderate them and bring them under the power of reason. And so it should be evident that there is no possibility of beginning too early with religious culture, providing we mean by it Christ and his spirit and temper. Everything of an abstract nature, and especially everything controversial must be postponed. Jesus — what he was, what he said, what he did; this is all that a child needs, and it really does seem as though God had made special provision in the method of the New Testament literature, in its parables and miracles for the child's nature. While the deepest meaning is profound enough for the philosopher, the surface teaching is simple enough for the child.

But I must not take liberties with your attention, although no theme is of greater practical importance, and none deserves more thorough treatment.

So long as we are in fetters to the idea that religion has its seat in the intellect, so long the children of our day will be defrauded of their rights in the kingdom of Christ. When once we are converted to the scriptural position that the seat of religion is in the affectional region, then children will begin to have their souls recognized as well as their bodies; never till then. The intellectual view of religion limits God's relation to the soul of man. It limits the sphere of the operation of the Spirit of God. It limits the area of Christ's atonement by virtually making it depend on intellectual apprehension, thus confining its results to adult life. It limits and pauperizes human nature. It puts religion on the same level with mathematics, biology, geology, philosophy, something to be acquired mentally. It makes God's will to be limited by man's will, and makes the Almighty wait as a servant at man's door to ask permission of his creature to begin his work on the soul. Thus, this intellectual view of religion is dishonoring to man and God both. The Ptolemaic system of astronomy was superseded generations ago. The Ptolemaic system of religion remains still — man with his proud intellect at the centre, not God with his unchanging love. When our Lord took a little child and set him in the midst of the disciples and said that that little child was the greatest in the Kingdom of Heaven, He, by that act, overturned the religion of mere intellectualism and established a religion in which the affectional was uppermost. The affectional was predominant in that child. Greatness always has its seat in the affections. There never yet was a great nature in which the affectional was not predominant. Of course if there be no affection in your child there *can* be no religion. And the depth, the strength, the force, the fervor, the glow of religious conviction in any soul will be in exact relation to the depth, the force, the strength of the affection in that soul. Selfishness, scheming, and calculation eat out the capacity for religiousness in a soul because they eat out its capacity for affection.

Let us not forget that there is only one beginning to any life, and everything in the life begins then. You cannot begin a religious life at forty or fifty without beginning it under disadvantages which are serious. Nor can you begin it at twenty without some disadvantages that need not be. The beginnings of religion or irreligion are in the earliest years, and long before its existence is recognized. Even Calvin, speaking of infancy, says, "The work of God in the soul is not without existence because it is unobserved and not understood by us." We forget that everything that is in manhood is in germ in childhood — everything. There is nothing added in after years, no new faculty, no new power. It is all there from the first. And that which is strongest in manhood is that which has been fed and tutored into predominance. The whole Kingdom of Christ lay folded up in that babe at Bethlehem. It was there in its quietest, its gentlest and sweetest expression. And in every babe there is religious capacity. If not, in the babe there will never be in the man. Oh then, do not sin against the child. Do not rob it of its place in the family. Do not defraud it of its birthright. As soon as it can know anything let it know that it has a father and mother on earth because it has a father in Heaven, a Deliverer from all evil in Jesus the Christ, let this be the basis truth on which its nature is built. And then if in the stormy years of temptation that follow, it should ever be tempted to the folly and madness of the prodigal, and leave the shelter of a Father's House to spend its substance in riotous living, there is a hope, amounting almost to an assurance, that when it comes to itself, the first truth it knew will assert its power and the erring soul will turn its footsteps back with the resolve, "I will arise and go to my Father and will say unto him, 'Father I have sinned against Heaven and before thee, and am no more worthy to be called thy son.'"

X.

A MORE EXCELLENT WAY.

> But covet earnestly the best gifts. And yet shew I unto you a more excellent way.— 1 *Cor.*, xii: 31.

THESE words of the Apostle have a backward and a forward look. There is the way which he has just trodden and the "more excellent way" which he is about to show. We must know both ways before we can estimate the greater excellency of the one over the other. Searching into the chapter at the very end of which are the words of our text, what do we find as its theme? "Now concerning Spiritual gifts." These words contain it. Following, step by step, the leading of the Apostle's thought, we learn that these men and women to whom he writes had been Gentile idolators, much in the same condition of mind and life as we find the Hindoos and Chinese to-day. But they had been changed from this condition, had been converted as we say, and were disciples of Christ. The Apostle attributes this discipleship to the operation of the Holy Spirit of God upon their minds. "No man speaking by the Holy Spirit, (under His influence) calleth Jesus anathema, and no man can say that Jesus is the Lord but by the Holy Spirit." And that which was true of these men and women of Corinth is equally true of us. If Jesus Christ be Lord to us we have the evidence in ourselves of having been and being under the power of the Holy Spirit of God. Then the Apostle proceeds to speak of spiritual gifts, the results of the unseen operation of the Spirit of God as manifested in the Christian church of that day. There would naturally be among new converts a propensity to assume that some one class of gifts was orthodox and others questionable. Perplexity and confusion would arise. And so the Apostle warns them against 'limiting the Holy One of Israel.' He tells them there are 'diversities of gifts,' 'differences of administration,' that as in material nature so in spiritual nature, *variety* is not inconsistent with unity. One man is wise, he has excellent judgment; another man seems to have an intuitiveness of knowledge; another man has strong faith; another the gift of healing; another the gift of prophecy; another can work miracles; another discerns spirits; another has the gift of tongues; and still another the interpretation of tongues. Now, we cannot stay this morning to inquire particularly as to the nature of these gifts, how far they were the quickening of the natural by the intense action of the supernatural upon it, so that each gift followed the law of the natural propensity of the individual, that or something else. All that is necessary to our purpose is to point to the truth emphasized by the Apostle, that the power underneath all, was the self-same Spirit of God, and that the Sovereignty of God was shown in the distribution and operation of the gifts, "dividing to every man severally *as He will.*"

The Apostle goes on to show that the diversity is not simply consistent with Unity, but required in order to Unity. Oneness is not unity. Individualism is not unity. Many there be who contend for the unity of the Godhead, but all the while they mean the Individualism of the Godhead. Unity comes of diversity. The Apostle illustrates this by reference to the human body. The foot, the hand, the ear, the eye, the members, are all different. The eye cannot hear. The ear cannot see. The foot has no ability of doing the work of the hand. Every part has its own special office, and the total result is not schism but unity. If the hand were to put out the eye the hand itself would be a loser. Pain in one part means discomfort everywhere. Each part serves every other part, and serves it all the more effectively by being different from it. "Whether one member suffer, all the members suffer with it; or one member be honored all the members rejoice with it." This is so in the material body which the Apostle uses as an illustration and suggests his ideal of a perfect church, though the ideal be far ahead of present attainment. In the church there are Apostles, but *all* are not apostles; there are teachers, but *all* men are not teachers; there are times of miracle, but *all* times are not conditioned for the miraculous; there are gifts of healing, but very few men have them, *all* do not speak with tongues, *all* have not the interpretation of tongues, and yet some have. These are the gifts, in all their manifold variety, all when genuine and true tending towards unity. These gifts have been of great value to the church. Those we differentiate by the word 'miraculous' belong to times when, without some unquestioned sign of the Divine presence and power, men could not stand before the terrific opposition brought to bear against them. There are ages in which the excellency of a thing is not enough to win acceptance for it, ay, ages in which the more supernal the excellency, the more violent will be the opposition. In such ages men and their message have to be protected by some such aureole of glory as only God Himself can throw around their brows. Miracles, wonders and signs are not so much for the conviction of the unbeliever as for the protection of the believer. We do not find that even the raising of Lazarus was of much, if any use, for evangelistic purposes. Men only deceive themselves when they assume that their disposition Godward would be changed by any visitations from the world of spirits. If there be anything in what is called " Spiritualism " it is certain that its effect has been all the other way. It has demoralized men instead of promoting in them holy character. And so, while the miracles of our Lord were revelations of Divine Power and of a Kingdom of Heaven, while they overawed many unbelievers, they did not convert them.

Now, in these days of ours, we are often in a state of rebellion because we cannot command signs and wonders. God's promises are that he will come down " as rain upon the mown grass," "as showers that water the earth," " I will be as the dew unto Israel " a gentle, constant, fructifying influence. But we want freshets to bear away the bridges, and make a loud report. We have very little faith in what our Lord Himself says, that " the Kingdom of God cometh not with observation." We want Pentecost, with its tongues of flame, and its mighty rushing wind, but are we ready for the outside persecutions, the tortures, the deaths, the Herodian tyrannies and all the terrific opposition which in the one direction corresponded to Pentecost in the other? Pentecost was God's answer to man's demoniac hatred. No men, without a Pentecostal baptism, would have dared to face such a frowning world as that which glared upon the Apostles. And when you and I are called to face the fires of martyrdom we shall have Pentecostal power in which to face them. It is enough for all ordinary purposes if our Lord be with us "as the dew," "as the rain," "as the showers that water the earth," if we live spiritually in a dispensation of the Spirit as we live naturally in a dispensation of the sunlight. Our God never acts arbitrarily. Not only the times and the seasons, but the spiritual proprieties and necessities of the times and seasons are in His hand and under His sovereign control. He giveth to every age as to every man, "severally as He will."

And now I want that we should specially notice that this Apostle says there is "a more excellent way" to the attainment of the end sought by God, than this way of miracle and wonder and sign. He says, "seek earnestly the best gifts," but the time will come when it will appear that these gifts are inferior to something else. The time will come when speaking with tongues, gifts of healing, working miracles, all these signs and wonders will be seen as provisional and temporary. In the very nature of things they cannot be continued. Their continuation would make them commonplace. They would lose their uses and cease to be of service. That which God seeks for man can be accomplished when the world is ready for it by some agency whose permanency will not make it commonplace — viz., by the existence and cultivation of that state of heart which is expressed in the one word " charity." It is a very remarkable thing, and will appear more and more noteworthy, the longer we ponder it, that this Apostle, living in the time of miracle and wonder and sign, and able to estimate the exact result of these, should yet boldly subordinate them, as evangelistic agencies, to the power of Christian charity, giving them an inferior and temporary place. These Pentecostal manifestations, for which we so often sigh, thinking, in our ignorance that if only we had them, the supremacy of the church as a Divine Institute would be universally acknowledged, and " a nation born in a day," St. Paul counts as provisional and inadequate to the ends which, we assume, they would further. We want something for the eye, something for the ear, something sensuous, the Kingdom of God coming with observation. Better than all these if only you could get it, says the Apostle, would be charity — that Christian love which is the strongest and most powerful of all Divine creations. " For though I speak with the tongues of men and of angels, and have not charity, I am become as sounding brass and tinkling cymbals. And though I have the gift of prophecy and understand all mysteries and all knowledge; and though I have all faith, so that I could remove mountains, (for there is tremendous energy in faith) and have not charity, I am nothing." He goes further still, and John the Baptist like, lays the axe to the root of the tree.—" Though I bestow all my goods to feed the poor, and though I give my body to be burned and have not charity, it profiteth me nothing." This is startling doctrine, startling, but undeniably Apostolic. A man may have these gifts referred to, and yet may fall short of having attained to any possession of the central thing in Christianity, that which distinguishes it from every false religion, and every corrupt form of a true religion the world has ever known. Men may have the energy of faith and very little if any charity. What seems stranger still, they may be large and liberal givers of money to the poor, and not have charity. They may even go to the martyr's stake and not have charity. All donations of money are not acts of charity. All martyr-deaths are not evidences of pure love to God and love to man. Many a man has been so self-willed, and so consumed with passion, so obstinate that he would rather die than give in. Many a man has willed away money to the poor simply because he could not hold it any longer, or because the solicitation was too urgent, or because he must save appearances, or because his conscience was not very easy as to the way in which he obtained his money. For as one has recently said in a published exposition of the Lord's Prayer, when we pray, "Give us this day *our* daily bread," *our* bread. "Bread that we beg is not ours; bread that we take as lazy pensioners on some one else's bounty, is not ours; bread that we steal is not ours; bread that we get from other people by fraud and extortion and over-reaching is not ours; only the bread that we have earned by honest work and fair traffic is ours." That which a man gives heartily and lovingly is perfumed with the incense of charity — not that which he gives grudgingly and of necessity.

I dare not take liberties with your time, and therefore it is not possible for me to enter into any adequate analysis as to what this charity, exalted to the highest place and to the grandest power by this Apostle, is. All we can say about it is, that whatever "suffereth long and is kind, whatever envieth not, whatever vaunteth not itself and is not puffed up, whatever doth not behave itself unseemly, whatever seeketh not her own, and is not easily provoked, whatever disposition is in any of us to think good and not evil, always putting us on the side of the best construction of a deed and not the worst, whatever does not rejoice in iniquity, whatever rejoiceth in the truth, whatever beareth all things, believeth all things (good that is), hopeth all things, and endureth all things," that is charity. The opposite of all these is not charity. Charity is inconsistent with petulance, with unkindness, with envy, with boasting and self-conceit and self-importance, with unseemliness in behavior, with the attributing of evil motive, with self-seeking, and all these ugly and evil things. A man may have *zeal* and no charity, yea *faith* enough to be very energetic and have no charity, have sundry useful gifts and no charity. Charity is eternal, undying, everlasting; it never faileth. The nearest thing on earth to it is a mother's love. It is the atmosphere of the society of Heaven. It is the dominating characteristic of redeemed, godlike souls. It gives a certain type and flavor of character wherever it exists. It gives to the mind broadness and comprehensiveness. It gives to the heart tenderness and loveableness. It is the concentrated essence of all the Evangelistic forces that have ever been in the church from the first day of its life to the day that now is.

And if the Church of Christ were richly dowered with the will and ability to tread this more excellent way it would not need to sigh for Pentecostal *signs* and *wonders*. Its power would be irresistible. But it would be the power of life, not the mechanical power of any ecclesiastical instrument that has ever been formed or can be.

By means of artificial heat, kindled in glowing furnaces, with the frost shut out, it is possible to have flowers and fruits in winter, but when once the summer sun pours down its June rays no artificial contrivances are needed. And so when once there is the reality of the religion of Jesus, the Divine charity of which this inspired Apostle speaks, the excellency of the way will be perceived. Some there be who ever cry, "we want more faith." But faith, my brother, cannot be a substitute for charity, and can perennially live only in an atmosphere charged with charity, as plants in an atmosphere charged with oxygen.

Others say we want more *zeal*, but zeal may be only like a galvanic battery moving the muscles of a corpse. Charity will do all and everything that zeal can do, or that faith can do, or that tongues can do, or that even miraculous gifts can do. And yet how few believe it. But no man, without twisting Scripture, can deny the Apostolicity of the teaching.

Who then, in the light of this teaching, are the men and women who are most truly representative of the church of Christ, who really embody its spirit, and carry forward its work? The answer can only be — they who have the charity of which the Apostle speaks. Paul and John were the greatest apostles because they were most richly dowered with charity.

XI.

THE PRE-EMINENCE OF CHRIST.

"That in all things he might have the pre-eminence."—*Col.*, i: 18.

NO one reading the opening passages of this letter of the great Apostolic letter-writer can be in doubt as to the estimate he formed of the personality of Jesus; his mind and heart are so possessed with Him that all things in heaven and earth are viewed as having their interpretation in Him. The Eternal One is spoken of as "the Father of our Lord Jesus Christ." That is enough for the mind of Paul. That is all he wants to know. All creation cannot tell as much of God as is told in the simple fact that He was "the Father of our Lord Jesus Christ." The mind of Paul is at rest as regards the Divine disposition towards him. His awe remains, but all base fear has gone. There is happiness enough in this one fact, that he and those to whom he wrote had been "delivered out of the power of darkness and translated into the Kingdom of the Son of his love." And then he proceeds to heap up thought upon thought as though he could not get the inward feeling into anything like adequate utterance. "In Him we have redemption," "In Him we have forgiveness of sins," "He is the image of the invisible God," He is "the first-born of every creature." "In Him were all things created, in the heavens and upon the earth — things visible and things invisible — whether thrones or dominions or principalities, or powers; all things have been created unto Him and through Him; He is before all things; in Him all things are held together.

He is the head of the body, the church, who is the beginning, the first-born from the dead, that in all things he might have the pre-eminence. For it was the good pleasure of the Father that in Him should all the fulness dwell; and through Him to reconcile all things unto Himself, having made peace through the blood of his cross; through Him I say, whether things upon the earth or things in the heavens."

I would like to ask Paul what he meant by some of these utterances. It takes a Paul fully to interpret a Paul. But this much we may say, without any possibility of being in the wrong, that to the Apostle Paul Jesus Christ was immeasurably more than He is to you and me. Great natures are certain to be the depositaries of great ideas, great feelings, great hopes, great aspirations. Greatness does not mean bulkiness. It means the ability of thinking great thoughts, letting in great ideas, following in the line of great aspirations and doing it continuously as long as life shall last. It is a question whether upon earth a greater man has ever lived than the writer of this letter. He has been before the world, with his bundle of letters, for 1800 years, and every generation of Christians has found Him ahead of them. I question whether there be a man living who can say as much about Jesus Christ in the same number of words as St. Paul has said in that passage I have read.

I think, however, that if there be any one expression which holds in it all the rest, it is this, "that in all things he might have the pre-eminence." Let us analyze this pre-eminence and see in what it consists:—

1. He is pre-eminent as to His personality. In the midst of all who have ever been in this world, He stands *unique* as to human character;—leaving out, for the moment, all thought of everything that rises above the human; if we had time to go into a detailed search after all the elements in His make-up to which the word *human* could properly be applied, we should be compelled to say that He is pre-eminently human. He came into the world through the gateway of the Hebrew nation,

and yet He is not a Jew. He belonged, so far as time could put a date upon Him, to the period of 1880 years ago, and yet He is of no age. He spent His days and nights under those insufferably bright eastern heavens, and yet He is of no clime. As we study His character, and then study the records of character which have come down to us of other peoples, we are obliged to confess that He gathers up into Himself all the best elements in Jewish life, in Grecian life, in Roman life. The characteristic Hebrew elements were such as we indicate by the words, "moral" and "devotional." Grecian life was elegant, refined and sensuous. It was occupied with feelings of natural beauty. Roman life was swayed by ideas of law, of empire and world-wide dominion. Your memory will furnish you with illustrative passages in proof of what I say that all these ideas were in the mind of Jesus Christ, not excluding or controverting one another, or jostling one another, but holding fellowship one with another. They were there in their purest and best expression. We need not stay upon the proof that He was pre-eminently moral and devotional; enemies as well as friends admit that. But He was devotional without being formal, and moral without any approach to prudishness. But how about His gathering up into Himself the best elements in Grecian life? Search and see how all things beautiful affect Him.

"Behold the lilies how they grow, they toil not, neither do they spin, and yet I say unto you that even Solomon in all his glory, was not arrayed like one of these." His love for country scenes, never once sleeping in a city; His retirement into the recesses of nature for devotional and teaching purposes; His unconcealed admiration of the white marble temple which rose lustrous and massive in the midst of the squalor of the streets of Jerusalem, His love of garden beauty, His constant use of natural symbols to illustrate His teachings, these are evidence enough of His being in sympathy with all that was beauteous, a very Greek for sensitiveness. But how about His gathering up into Himself all the best elements in the life of Rome, its appreciation of law and rule and dominion? His glorification of the moral law; and His refusal to utter one word that would be seditious, though a Cæsar was on the throne, His ready payment of the usual poll-tax when asked of Him and His disciples, these are sufficient to illustrate the first. And but one quotation is necessary to prove the truth of the assertion that with all that was pure and great in the aspirations of Rome, for Empire and world-wide dominion He was in sympathy. With Rome it was the simple ambition for power, with Jesus the aspiration of universal benevolence—a sympathy with all men everywhere, and thus a burning desire to bring them under the rule of One God and Father, that universal brotherhood might be established. "When the Son of man shall come in His glory and all His Holy angels with Him, then shall He sit upon the throne of His glory and before Him shall be gathered all nations." Thus we see how pre-eminent was His personality. He was neither Jew, nor Greek, nor Roman, and yet all that was distinctive and characteristic in Jew and Greek and Roman was illustrated in Him.

2. Then again he was pre-eminent as to his ideas of God and man. Let me say that this is always the test of pre-eminence of nature, largeness of idea on these two all-absorbing themes. The man who is pre-eminently great and good, will necessarily have the most ennobling ideas on these two themes. And you may be very sure that the instinct in our nature to regard with suspicion and distrust the Satanic school who first of all, deprive God of His personality, and then man of his spirit, is ingrained and inborn. It is the same kind of instinct which the dove has when the bird of prey comes into sight. If any one says "It is only an instinct of self-preservation," what of it? Is not that saying a great deal? If there were no lust of sinning in our nature, and no desire to have doubts enough to allow us to do it unrestrainedly, there is not an Infidel Lecturer in the world who could pay his travelling expenses

out of his earnings. The right idea of God is
always an inspiration to a good man; it is a
restraint, a fetter on an evil man. Jesus Christ
came specially to give us right ideas of the nature
of God and man. The idea He gave us of God
was pre-eminent. No one had ever approached
it. To be able to utter it and live it, gives this
Jesus a pre-eminence as a thinker who personalized his own thinking as no one else ever did.
He gave us an idea of God that made God " an
absolutely new being to our race." There had
been many attempts to name God, to put the
nature of God into a word, but every attempt had
fallen short of this which Jesus made, and must
fall short, for the reason that it takes a Jesus
Christ to give such utterance to the word
"*Father*" as shall make it mean what it does
mean. Words are variable as to their quality and
quantity, according to the quality and quantity of
the speaker. The words of Scripture on your
lips and mine — how poverty-stricken, compared
with the same words as spoken by Jesus of
Nazareth! So much of religious effort has been
occupied in emptying the words of Jesus of their
spiritual content, that they may be made to fit the
poverty of our ideas. "The thought of an Eternal Father, ruling in love, through righteousness,
towards lovely and righteous ends — that thought
of the Eternal, brooding in ceaseless pity, working

in untiring energy in all the units for the good alike of the single person and the collective race, that idea was the splendid gift of Christ to man." There was never any such large idea of God in the world before Christ came, but since, such ideas have been struggling into form, and other ideas which naturally flow from them, and now men who make no confesssion of mental and spiritual allegiance to Christ are often found uttering thoughts which had no existence in the speech of the world in Anti-Christian times. Infidel minds are sometimes found clothed in raiment of Christian ideas, and are innocently unconscious from whence they have plagiarized their clothes. Indeed, as one has said, "Christ's idea of God has so entered into and possessed the spirit of man that he cannot expel it or escape from it. It is now His, even in spite of Himself, for ever."

Add to the idea which Jesus has given us of the nature of God, His idea of the nature of man. In the Anti-Christian days the noblest man among the Jews was the chief of the Pharisees or the chief of the Sadducees. Among the Greeks the noblest man was the most physically beautiful man, the Apollo Belvidere was the type of him. Among the Romans the noblest man was one of the type of Julius Cæsar, the simply strong man, the man of achievement, though in order to achieve he trampled everyone who was in his path in the dust. How is it now in Christian lands? Under the influence of Jesus, the noblest man is not simply the bravest man, but "the gentlest, the humanest, the chastest, and the most charitable." It is a new idea of man, and entirely Christian in its completeness. *This* kind of man is man with the lost image restored. This kind of man must be immortal, for the life of the immortal God is in him. Why should he die? He is in harmony with the Universe. Everything in it conspires to say to him, live; and to help him to live. And so the revelation of Immortality naturally and necessarily comes with the emergence into being of this Christian type of man. It takes an immortal spirit to hold in it the idea of immortality.

Take one or two other *ideas* characteristically Christian which will help us to see how pre-eminently Christ Jesus is the world's greatest thinker as well as holiest man. The idea of the universal brotherhood of man; the idea that love of God is expressed in service of man; the idea that the original image of God, though lost to sight in so many, may be latent in the worst, a jewel at the centre of a dung-heap;—these are ideas floating up and down the world to-day, and wherever they enter the soul of man, entering it to stay, and making men restless until society is harmonized with these ideas. Many men wilfully refuse to live under the shadow of this Tree of Life, Jesus Christ, but unconsciously they are eating of the fruit of the tree. Viewed intellectually as well as morally, this Jesus of Nazareth has the pre-eminence. His ideas of God and man are immeasurably vaster than any other ideas which have been flung into the world's life. Intellectually He has the pre-eminence.

And yet once more He is pre-eminent as to His mission in the world. No other ever came on such a mission; no other was ever capable of entertaining the idea of it. The very conception of such a mission puts Him into the place of pre-eminence. What was it? To bring a revolted world back again into allegiance. Think for a moment what that means. Into allegiance — into such allegiance as is worthy of God to accept, and of man to give. Not forced allegiance. Not the allegiance which the conqueror gets when the commander-in-chief on the other side delivers up his sword. Not simply the allegiance which the slave, beggared in spirit as in everything else, gives to the Master whom he has no power to resist — No, no such allegiance is unworthy of a God to receive. Nothing satisfies love but love, nothing satisfies reason but that which is endorsed by reason, nothing satisfies sincerity but sincerity, and so it would be unworthy of God to receive from man anything short of that sincere, reasonable, intelligent, loving allegiance, which is the only true allegiance. But we need not complicate the matter, wherever there is one spark of real love all else follows. And so we hear our Lord saying in justification of His receiving the sinning woman, "Her sins which are many are all forgiven for she loved much."

To bring a world into this sincere, reasonable, intelligent, loving allegiance towards God is the mission which Jesus the Christ set Himself. It is either the work of a God or of a madman. But as a madman could never even conceive of such a mission, the conception in itself shows the pre-eminence of the nature in which it dwelt.

The accomplishment of this mission seems to you and me impossible. Think what is involved in it. Nay, you cannot. We often use the word "regeneration," but we know not what it implies. It is a word expressing some spiritual process which lies out of the region of our observation. We know the signs of it, but of the process we know nothing. When a man adheres through all temptations and persecutions, through all the flatteries of prosperity, and the despondencies of adversity to the Christ of God as his Redeemer and Savior, we know that he is regenerated. When like Job, he says, (meaning it), "though he slay me, yet will I trust in him," we know he is regenerated. But *when* and *how*, that we know not. We say, by the power of the Holy Spirit of God, because it is so revealed, and because it must be by a power greater than the human, greater than any power that man can exert. Yet this is the mission which this Jesus has undertaken: to regenerate the alienated heart of manhood, to bring it in loving, glad allegiance to the throne of God. Knowing what man is, knowing, as Solomon said ages ago, that "a brother offended is harder to be won than a strong city," knowing how much the human will can endure and not bend, knowing how even a prejudice, when it gets into a human spirit, can hold out against the strongest arguments, the most forcible reasons, the most persistent acts of benevolence and kindness — knowing all this, does it not seem more easily possible to swing the Universe out of its orbit, destroy its balance, and bring back chaos and old night, than to accomplish this restoration to loving allegiance of the alienated heart of man? Certainly this Jesus Christ must see in the deeps of man's nature more than we see, and He must know of forces in the spiritual realm, behind this material realm, stronger and more persuasive than we know of. Leaving all that is merely speculative, we assert that the very conception of such a mission puts this Jesus Christ pre-eminently above all other men who have ever lived on this earth.

The theme is only half finished, not half

indeed, for I have given you nothing more than a few suggestions, but I must leave it. It is only a portrait in outline, nay, not so much, only a few sketchy strokes.

If only it helps any human soul struggling into the light, any soul fighting the billows of doubt and trying to get to land, to some *terra firma* on which the foot can rest, it will not be in vain that we have tried to make it clear how in His personality, in the greatness of His ideas of God and man, and in His mission to this world, this Jesus Christ was not simply eminent as many men have been, but emphatically and unapproachably pre-eminent. A theology of abstract ideas is no theology at all. It is but the shadow of a theology. The substance is elsewhere. A theology which has not in it, in the place of pre-eminence, the person, the ideas, the mission of Christ is chaff and not bread. And so while we cannot measure the nature of Christ, if only we can see that He is pre-eminent in these particulars I have specified, we have enough for a foundation for all the religion of which our nature is capable.

I know of but one conspicuous man in the world of literature, the bitterness of whose malignity was such as to blind his eyes to all moral and spiritual beauty and allow him to cry out "*Ecrasez l' infame*" — Crush the wretch. If that man lives on in eternity no other punishment could surely be asked by his bitterest enemy than that it should be for ever remembered that he used those words in writing of Jesus the Christ.

Other great sceptics have seen the pre-eminence and have acknowledged it; as though God employed one sceptic to shame another. Even Rousseau, "that soul ever floating between error and truth," lost its hesitation, and with a hand firm as a martyr's, forgetting his age and his works, the philosopher wrote with the pen of a theologian a page which was to become the counterpoise of Voltaire's blasphemy, and concluded it with words which will resound throughout Christendom until the last coming of Christ, "If the life and death of Socrates be those of a saint, the life and death of Jesus Christ are those of a God."

Even Napoleon I.—the embodiment of militaryism, the old Roman back again in the Christian centuries, meditating on men and things in the lonely isle of St. Helena—cannot keep his mind off this man and His history. The fallen conqueror asks one of the few companions of his captivity if he could tell him what Jesus Christ really was. The soldier begged to be excused. He had been too busy in the world to think about that question. "What! you have been baptized in the Catholic church and cannot tell me what Jesus Christ was? Well, then, I will tell you." Then the man of Austerlitz and Jena began speaking of the great generals and emperors and conquerors of the world and ended with these words, "In fine, I know men, and I say that Jesus Christ was not a man." And so Goethe, the great literary dandy among men of genius, confesses Christ's pre-eminence when he says, "the moral majesty, the spiritual culture in the gospels can never be excelled." And so Schiller when he names the religion of Jesus "the Incarnation of the Holy;" and even Strauss acknowledges His pre-eminence when he praises Him as the "supreme religious genius of time;" and Renan too, diseasedly self-conscious as he ever is, confesses that He merits Divine rank. And so in all things, and from all sorts of men, St. Paul's words have been and are being fulfilled, "that in all things He might have the pre-eminence." Has He it in our hearts? Then to us belongs the joy that St. Paul felt when he uttered the words —"who hath delivered us out of the power of darkness and translated us into the Kingdom of the Son of His love."

XII.

OUR RELATIONSHIPS.

"At the hand of every man's brother will I require the life of man—*Genesis*, ix: 5.

THE subject of the Inspiration of the Old Testament Scriptures has often been in debate. Such debate every generation of men has to take part in. It is natural for us to accept the teachings of those who are in parentage to us, natural and right. So long as we are children we are under tutors and governors. These tutors and governors have to do their duty by us according to the best light they have. But the inevitable period of self-assertion comes. We arrive at the time when we have a right to our own individuality. The mind is conscious of itself. The generation ahead of us has to endure oftentimes a disagreeable amount of self-assertion. Examine into things for ourselves we must. It is an anxious time for those who have had the responsibility for us. Our inclination towards scepticism or faith will depend now upon the moral forces at the back of us and in us. Our opinions will be colored by our sympathies. If there be in us a natural goodness this period of debate is not dangerous. Of many a young man you hear it said by those who know him best, "oh, never fear, he'll come out right." Of others, "I'm not so sure about him," with a significant shake of the head. There is another kind of young man concerning whom not even so favorable a view as that is expressed. It is at this period of life that such questions as that of the inspiration of the Scriptures come up. And generally external evidence is thought to be that which is necessary to prove it. And so there is a great marshalling of facts and evidences which establish the probability. At this age the eye is not wide open to the *internal* evidence. It is not perceived that that is the strongest, and that without it all *external* evidence is well nigh useless. When you see outside the walls of a building a number of props to keep those walls from falling, there needs no other evidence of a bad foundation or wretchedly poor building. External evidence is often like propping up an ill-constructed and dishonestly built house. It is like asking a young student to supply you with proof that Agassiz was a great naturalist or that Descartes was a great philosopher. Agassiz and Descartes must supply the evidence themselves; no one else can do it. And so it is always. You cannot prove by any external evidence that Beethoven was a great composer, or Homer a great poet. These men must supply the evidence themselves. And so you cannot prove the inspiration of the Scriptures by any external process simply. Nor can you by *any* process to the mind not itself capable of receiving high inspirations. This is forgotten, that the mind of the individual must be itself capable of receiving inspiration from that in which inspiration dwells, or all attempts at proof are necessarily defective.

A blind man can receive no impulse from the verdure of nature, the blush of the rose, the delicacy of the lily, or the blue of the sky. A deaf man is not soothed when the music of "Oh, rest in the Lord, wait patiently for Him," falls upon the ear. It finds no entrance to his soul. The "Hallelujah Chorus" wakes no triumph in his heart. And so it is in relation to the inspiration of Scripture. If it cannot inspire me, move me, rouse something in me into response, you cannot prove to me its inspiration. Now when I find a declaration like this at the very threshold of the history of man's life " At the hand of every man's brother will I require the life of man," I feel the inspiration. How did this cosmopolitan truth get there? If it sprung up out of the soil of man's nature, then man was in an exceedingly advanced spiritual condition. Why, we are not up to it now. It is ahead of all but the most spiritually minded Christians. No other people are abreast of it. It is Pauline in its character. It would not surprise us to find it among the words of St. John in the ripeness of his old age. But to meet it in the early chapters of the Book of Genesis,— it creates something of the feeling which arose in the heart of a friend of mine who in the huts of a tribe of Maoris in New Zealand came upon a face like to some of the most beautiful he had seen in his native Scotland, and addressing her found that she was Scotch, but how she had got there he could not discover. And here we find a Christian truth of the most advanced kind in the opening of the book of Genesis: a truth which inspires every inspirable Christian heart, and so proves its own inspiration. "At the hand of every man's brother will I require the life of man."

The terms of the passage are too general to make any narrowing of them down within family limits legitimate. They contain the very advanced truth that every man belongs to every other man; that there is but one great human family; and that our action is not according to the will of God when it is conducted on lines of exclusion. Whether we see it or not the fact is everywhere assumed in Scripture, that that which is good for the whole humanity is good for each member of it.

Our policy is to be broadly sympathetic. In church, in state, religiously, politically, everywhere. The charge is put upon us to preserve human life, not simply our own individual life, but to do all we can to preserve human life everywhere. And this is every man's duty. I beseech you to notice how singularly inclusive as well as how unlimited the terms of this passage are :— "At the hand of every man's brother will I require the life of man —" I know not how words could be better ordered so as to prevent any of us finding a way of escape from their inclusiveness.

"The life of man," what is it? The true human life, what is it? That which is fitting and proper to you and me and all men, what is it? Because *that* is the life we have to preserve. We are not allowed to live in the front of great human problems we never so much as touch with the tip of our finger. Almighty God will not have that. It is contrary to His idea of man and His responsibility. Whatever occurs in a community or nation we have some sort of relation to it; we have an interest in it. There was one sublime moment in the history of the Roman people when one of their orators lifted the whole crowd to a higher plane than common as he exclaimed, "I am a man, nothing that is human is foreign to me." Overstepping all individual interests and all selfish feeling, leaping all bounds of place and time, he embodied in that one sentence the noblest aspiration that had ever moved in the heart of the noblest Roman citizen.

But how many, how very many, even now, in these Christian times, live on a very much lower plane than that! How often do we find ourselves saying, "It's no concern of mine whether people are this, that, and the other; if only I can be let alone to do my own business and enjoy my own life, that is all I ask." But that is not all that God asks; it is not all of which our nature is capable; and every man is accountable to God for the capability within him. We live in a world indefinitely improveable. In a right condition of society we live in a world capable of supporting an almost countless population. Man is here, even according to his natural endowments, to dress it and to keep it. Society is capable of being very different from what it is. And God has put upon each generation the responsibility of moving this world towards a completeness never yet attained, towards an order never yet reached, towards a sympathetic co-operativeness of man with man never yet approached.

Now, in this movement the Christian Church has a very important place to fill, and for this simple reason that it is the Trustee of the truth which is to leaven the mass of human opinion and feeling. If some one else is in possession of more advanced truth, let them give it us. We have a right to it. We need it. It has not yet appeared that anyone has. Much talk has been of recent years as to the wonderful change which is to pass over the lot of men generally by the discoveries of Science. And it would be a very foolish attitude for Christian men to take,—that of depreciating anything which Science can do to improve the lot of men. But Science is occupied simply with material forces. It does not pretend to step beyond them, although it *has* to do it, but then it is not strictly scientific. Supposing that everything which the most enthusiastic scientific optimists predict should come to pass; supposing that our material life should have everything provided to make it comfortable — what does it amount to? The telegraph brings us into closer neighborhood to men at a distance. The telephone has a similar use. The steam-engine transports us at a quicker rate from here to elsewhere. The steam-ship ploughs the main in saucy independence of the winds without whose favor sailing ships can make no progress. There is more of movement, more knowledge, more stir, more expenditure of nervous energy. The people who have nothing to do in the world (so far as they have made discovery) can move about the surface of this broad earth more rapidly under the delusion that they are really doing something. Facilities for travel have promoted the vagabond spirit and made it a little more respectable.

The merchant finds his customers in China and Japan as well as at his own doors. And has to; for our very material progress, this very inventiveness for which we are noted, is multiplying our difficulties. The Secretary of the Treasury of the United States has just told us in his report that our manufactures can thrive no longer by simply supplying the home market. "We can produce much more and much faster than we can consume: the existing iron, woolen, and cotton mills would meet in six months, perhaps in a shorter time, all our home demands." Our fields grow more wheat, and produce more corn, than we can sell; our factories make more clothes than we can wear; our cattle yield more meat than we can eat. And yet we are not content, far from it, our discontent grows with our abundance. We are verifying on a large scale the truth of the words that "a man's life does not consist in the abundance of the things which he possesses." We need something else than material prosperity, to make material prosperity a blessing.

It becomes us to make a calm estimate of what science can do for us; to note its limitations, and how soon we reach them. It may give us houses in which we can get ventilation without draughts, a temperature that is comfortable without being enfeebling; it may attend properly to all sanitary matters; it may even keep us from being made universally dyspeptic by wholesale adulteration of that which we eat and drink, though that seems very far off. For, in regard to obtaining these things on which our physical health depends, perfectly free from everything that is deleterious, we are almost under the necessity of doing as he was advised to do who asked a Portugese wine grower how he was to obtain in his cellars in England a cask of pure Port wine. Said the man, "I would advise you to come here and see the grapes grow; and watch them in every stage until their juice is in the cask: then to keep your eye on that identical cask marked with your own mark, and never for a moment allow it out of your sight until you deposit it in your cellar. I know no other way than that." So much of our misery comes from physical causes that in speaking of the "life of man" it is necessary to recognize them, and our own relation to the causes of much of the misery of this human race. No man but he who is blind in perception and judgment can close his eyes to the fact that so very many of our miseries come from causes over which we have control, and it is our duty, as servants of God and as being charged with the responsibility referred to in the text, to remove them if we can. Let us welcome all that science can do for us, but let us remember that its limits are soon reached, and this also, that neither science nor anything else is of any use to those who are too ignorant or too indolent to use it. There are men within one hundred miles of this place who have built into their houses everything which the latest knowledge supplies; who can command the most scientific physicians in the land, who can have everything that money can buy, and yet there is many a laboring man earning his few dollars a week who is both healthier and happier than they are. It is little better than sheer nonsense to talk of science supplying everything that our life needs to make it comfortable. No life ever yields comfort to its possessor, until it is conformed to the idea which He had for it who originally gave it. Everything has its state of fixity and there is no content and no satisfaction until that state is reached. This is specially and emphatically true of the life of man. We are members of a great human race in every one of whom there is the feeling of something attainable which has not yet been attained. As to what the something is there is endless diversity of opinion. But when the Apostle says, "The whole creation groaneth and travaileth together in pain until now," he recognizes the inward life of man seeking after something not yet reached. And this is not true alone of the ungodly, it is true also of the godly, "And not only they but we ourselves also who have received the first fruits of the Spirit even we ourselves groan within ourselves, waiting for the adoption." And yet, in another place, speaking of himself alone, he says, "Not as though I had already attained, either were already perfect, but I follow after if that I may apprehend that for which I am apprehended of Christ Jesus." The Biblical view of life is very much higher than the man of the world's view, or the moral view, or the scientific view. Says Froude, speaking of Carlyle — these lines were often on his lips to the end of his life:

"It is an old belief
   That on some solemn shore,
Beyond the sphere of grief,
   Dear friends shall meet once more:

Beyond the sphere of time,
   And sin and fate's control,
Serene in changeless prime
   Of body and of soul

That creed I fain would keep,
   This hope I'll not forego;
Eternal be the sleep
   If not to waken so."

Now the church has something more to do than to take care of itself. Very little good can it do on the principle of simply caring for itself. It has to sound in the ear of humanity, of men everywhere, the truth that is in these words, "At the hand of every man's brother will I require the life of man." It has to illustrate by its spirit and temper and by its deeds this fact — that all men belong to all other men. Missionary it must be or die. When Israel of old, elected to a high service to the world, fell below the level of its calling — then said the Apostle, and he but spake the mind of God, "Lo! we turn to the Gentiles." The doctrine of election, about which there has been so much needless wrangle, does not refer to personal salvation. It has nothing to do with *that*. It refers to a service, to a purpose, to a mission. The people of Israel were elected to a special dignity and mission to the whole world. They fell below it. They did not "make their calling and election sure;" then the mission was put into other hands. And every nation has had some special mission to the world. When it has fallen below it, then its period of decay has begun and it has hurried to its doom. It is so of the church of Christ. That church has to declare God's ideas, God's favor, God's will to the world as these have come to us in Jesus. It has to live those ideas before the world and *thus* gradually but surely renew the world. It is to be the leaven in the meal. It must be that every man is accountable for the right use of the noblest ideas which ever came into his soul. Quench them he must not. Stifle them he must not. He must nourish them into growth, or his soul will be a graveyard in which are buried the murdered innocents which would have grown into manhood but for the strangling hand of his scepticism. And so, while I speak of the Church as the collective of all God-inspired souls, I beseech you to note that in our text there is no absorption of the individual into the mass. "At the hand of every man's brother will I require the life of man." The whole life of man concerns each of us — all of us. That is the truth at the base of universal suffrage. We are responsible for the high or low tone of the life of man in the community in which we live, in the town, in the city, in the state, in the nation. "At the hand of every man's brother will I require the life of man." Why, says one, should I be punished for what another man does? Because we are all partakers of one life, and are related, and are a family, and the law is that if one member suffer all the members shall suffer with it. And so, if there be small-pox in the poor streets, you who live in the better streets begin to be concerned, you don't ask what have I to do with that man's small-pox? You say to the authorities, "Get the man off to the hospital; disinfect his house. Go in and do it." But what right have you to enter that man's house and haul him away to the hospital? What right have you to send the health officer with his disinfectant? You see, your doctrine of individualism breaks down in presence of a contagious and desolating disease, and very properly so. But is it not a miserable confession to make, that we have to learn the doctrine of our relationship to others on the *lowest* side of it, because we will not recognize it on its *highest* side? Now, while we really do more as churches than is done by the unchurched in the community in regard to the men and women who are, through ignorance and shiftlessness, at a great disadvantage, yet as churches, we are apt to separate between the material and the spiritual and to say, "Our work is spiritual not material." But how can you separate these? You never saw a man's body walking on one side of the street while his spirit was walking on the other side. Soul and body are so closely married in this life that no one can divorce them. They act and react on each other. Organization does not produce life;—life produces organization. We cannot separate the material and the spiritual. The life of man is too much of a unit to allow us to do that. And, says the Almighty One, "At the hand of every man's brother will I require the life of man." We are parts of a nation's life. All *its* questions are *our* questions. All its struggles are *our* struggles. All its failures are our failures, all its triumphs are our triumphs. Not till the regenerated brotherhood of the Church rises above its sectisms and boldly puts itself in the fore-front of the nation's life as the truthteller, the Evangelizer, claiming the life of man for Christ and testing everything by the principles of life He has given us, does it do its duty or fulfill its mission. Of course, a man begins with his individual wants, but the man who takes no interest in any one but himself, and even when he is voting his vote on a great national occasion is still voting for self, regardless of the great life of man, is a man not affiliated to the cause of Christ in the world and his end is defeat. But "our Father hears the man who cries to Him, however clumsily, for light and strength to do his duty. He may be utterly puzzled, utterly downhearted; utterly hopeless; but in acting on the higher plane introduced to us in this text, he is baptized with the Holy Ghost and with fire. God meets his willingness and endows him with power. He begins to have a right judgment: to see clearly what he ought to do, and how to do it. He grows more clear-sighted, more prompt, more steady than he has ever been before. And there comes a fire into his heart such as he never had before, a spirit and a determination which nothing can daunt or break, which makes him bold, cheerful, earnest in the face of the anxiety and danger which would, at any other time, have broken his heart. The man is lifted up above his former self, and carried on through his work, he hardly knows how, till he succeeds nobly, or if he fails, fails nobly."

But the inspiration of the Spirit of God, meeting His willingness, makes him to see and feel that he is allied to the life of man. And he acts from a higher view and on a broader plane of things than before. He hardly knows himself again. Seeing farther, feeling more deeply, life enlarges to his vision, and you hear him hymning this glorious petition : —

> "Father, hear the prayer we offer,
> Not for ease that prayer shall be,
> But for strength, that we may ever
> Live our lives courageously."

To save life, not to destroy it, is thenceforth his aim, and whatever the line he take, whatever the work he do, according to his possessions, his opportunity, his talent, he realizes a blessedness unknown before, and to such an one there is no harrassing rebuke ever tormenting his soul even in words like these, "At the hand of every man's brother will I require the life of man."

XIII.

THE LIMITATIONS OF EVIL.

But I say unto you, my friends, Be not afraid of them that kill the body, and after that, have no more that they can do.— Luke, xii: 4.

IN those times when the air is full of war and rumors of war, "distress of nations with perplexity,— the sea and the waves roaring, men's hearts failing them for fear," — in such times men have to seek out some truth which shall help to steady the mind and keep it hopeful. For no man but he who is heartless can keep himself from shuddering at the idea of warfare, wholesale carnage, men mown down by hundreds and thousands, wives turned into widows, children made fatherless, mothers left to mourn their only sons, the tender humanities of life ruthlessly trodden under foot, the hard earned money of the people compulsorily exacted from them and spent for the direst purposes man knows, in doing devil's work, not the work of God. All this is terrible to look at and think of. How should we view it if we were introduced to it for the first time? If the history of man had not been one of warfare, if now the idea and the purpose of it were suddenly sprung upon us, what a howl of indignation there would be from one end of the world to the other against any one of any nationality who should propose to use Intellect and Science in preparing means and methods for man's destruction! In our unimpassioned moments we are all, surely, on the side of unwarlike statesmen, men who on their shoulders have the heaviest kind of responsibility, men who will do anything and everything that can be done rather than draw the sword. Such men have oftentimes to hear themselves charged with vacillation, cowardice, want of heroism, and I know not what else, but if you or I were in the place of such a man should we not do everything doable to make war impossible, and if we failed, to make it on behalf of those who were responsible for the failure criminal. In our day there are so many commercial interests which make a pecuniary profit out of war. These are clamorous all the time. Men who deal in money on stock-exchanges are clamorous too. And the newspapers, through which we get our information, have a pecuniary interest in war. These clamorous interests make it extremely difficult for statesmen, who are at heart peace-makers, to get a fair hearing or fair-play.

One of the blessings for which we cannot be too grateful, is that this continent from the Atlantic to the Pacific is not to be split up into rival nationalities, jealous of each others' power and progress, preyed upon by treacherous diplomats in league with professional soldiers who can get promotion only through war. The division between North and South would have been the open gateway to the introduction of all the old world evils to this continent. The perpetuation of the Union meant very much more than the perpetuation of the American idea, it meant the exclusion of the Italian and Spanish Machiavellian idea, the exclusion of the German imperial idea, the exclusion of the Russian autocratic idea, that the country is to be sacrificed to the interests of the Czar, the exclusion of the English aristocratic idea that God made the many for the sake of the few, all these ideas would have got footing and power and permanency here if the South had been allowed to assert and establish its independence. *Now*, the whole force of the national mind can be turned toward internal improvements, to the condition of the people generally and how to elevate it. The professional soldier becomes only a superior kind of policeman, the defender of personal liberty not the assailant of any one, as such to be respected and honored. We ask, however, will the time never come when the professional soldier shall be the soldier of Conscience and of Civilization and thus the embodiment of the Old Chivalry? Will he never be the man who prevents instead of foments war? Will the time never come when Christianity shall have conquered the militaryism of the civilized nations of the world, and when there shall among those nations be a holy league and covenant to prevent war? When a dog becomes mad everybody in the region is interested in preventing his biting men, women and children. And when a nation is suddenly seized with the war frenzy, all other nations should combine against it. There is no other way to make war the disgraceful and hateful thing it is. Despots, using huge armies for the avenging their own private quarrels with other despots, or for the promoting their own insatiable ambition, or for the creating interests outside the nation for the sake of calling off attention from the deplorable condition of things inside, these men should be given to understand that they have had their day, and for humanity's sake, must cease to be.

The New Testament is remarkable for its brief recognition of all the facts of life and its suggestions as brief, and effective, of thoughts which should bring some degree of comfort even in the presence of the direst difficulties and the most doleful degradations. While we cannot undertake to give anything that could be called an exhaustive interpretation of this text to which our attention is called, yet it introduces to us certain ideas which may, in times of trouble, be of some help and comfort to us.

The first of these ideas is this—that there is a limit to the power of evil. "Fear not them which kill the body, and after that have no more that they can do." It would appear to us in those moments in which we are most sympathetic, that there is nothing more diabolical than war. It has been characterized as the sum of all human villainies. Any form of government which makes war easy is condemned as in itself evil. No other word need be said. No apology for it ought for a moment to be listened to. Abolish it; for humanity's sake, abolish it. That form of government which in the nature of the case is most pacific, is the form which a God of Love must mean to exist. But even war is not the worst of evils. It would be better for men to go to war believing that they were doing something thereby for God and His Kingdom, than to have perpetual peace with no belief in God at all, just as it is better for a man to die in doing something that calls out the fulness of his life than for his powers to rot in indolence. That which Divine Providence permits here on this earth, is a part of the condition of human freedom. It is part of the discipline of life. But there is a limit even to the worst things that a man can do. When he murders me he comes to the limit of his ability. He releases my soul from its fetters, he unbinds me from this earth, he hurries me into the spiritual world. It is an immense thing to do for me; it may be, as far as I am personally concerned, a great blessing conferred; as far as the doer of the deed is concerned it must be the weightiest curse, for he has done his worst on me.

The Christian view of death does not make murder any the less of a crime, it does nothing to justify war, but it does a great deal to relieve our minds when we think upon Divine Providence. What meditative mind is there that has not been on the edge of disbelief in a Divine Providence in times of dire calamity, when human life seemed so cheap as almost to be worthless, blood poured out like water, and for what? To gratify human ambition, to avenge some fancied injury or slight, even to help depopulate a country because of angry growlings arising from internal discontent. Nine-tenths of the wars of the world have been criminal. They have been wars which have left nations sadder, poorer, more demoralized, than when they began. They have left behind them no stable government, no freed slaves, no possibilities of improvement, nothing of any value. And when we think of such wars and the men who are responsible for them, we can hardly refrain from thanking God for the words, "After death the judgment." No moral order could eternally exist in a universe in which such monstrosities and such monsters were not punished. And yet, looking all the facts of life full in the face, sympathizing as none other ever did with the myriads of torn and bleeding hearts which war has rent and broken, our Lord could say to us, "Fear not them which kill the body and after that have no more that they can do." He could say so because He knew the beyond. He saw the limit to evil. He saw the line beyond which it could not go. He was in the secret of the councils of the Almighty One who had said, "Thus far shalt thou go and no farther." It was not heartlessness which spoke. This is not the language of a soul devoid of sympathy, not the language of one capable of saying, "Let them go on with their wars, it will make it better for trade." Oh, no; nothing of this, it was the language of one who could march straight up to Calvary, who, hanging there, refused the anodyne that would have lulled His physical pain, because He saw clearly the beyond, and so, for the joy that was set before Him, endured the cross, despising the shame. Have we not a right to all the help His words give us? Nay; do not those who refuse this help, defraud themselves? It is impossible in the present developed state of the human mind, to believe in a

Divine providence apart from the revelation of Immortality. I think that I am justified in saying it is impossible to believe in it apart from the revelation of a judgment beyond the line we call death. One of the great intellectual arguments for the truth of the Christian doctrines is their coherence, the way in which they form a whole, the way in which one necessitates the other. The same Holy Spirit which convinces the mind of Sin, convinces it of a Righteousness which is absolute and of a Judgment which cannot be evaded or avoided. The three ideas cohere; they tenant the mind together. They belong to one another. In this state of existence man cannot develop without freedom, without a measure of freedom which seems to us dangerous, even, at times, appalling. The fact that a man should have the liberty and the power to kill his fellow man seems to us, when we are meditative, dreadful. The fact that it should be possible for men to organize armies for the express purpose of wholesale slaughter of each other seems more dreadful still. The attendant fact that men should be so capable of deluding themselves as to assume that on this field of slaughter, virtue and heroism can be most appropriately and conspicuously shown, is astounding. And yet there is no denial of the facts. Our Lord knew them as well as we know them; saw the battle-fields bristling with bayonets; the smoke of their artillery; the red of their carnage; heard the groans of dying men, and the moans of dying horses, heard it all, saw it all, shuddered at it all, and yet He could calmly say to us, "Fear not them which kill the body, and after that have no more that they can do." There is a limit to the power of evil. It is not almighty. It is not infinite. It has its sphere, and within that sphere can do its dire work. Murderers may murder the body; the aggressive military spirit may take up its abode in nations and get itself legalized and be made honorable even, but it is not of God. It may "kill the body, and after that it has no more that it can do."

The second idea, a still profounder idea, is this, that death is a rescue from all evils which are not demoniac in their character. It seems to me quite impossible to read the New Testament with that attention which it demands and deserves, and fail to notice that there are two kinds of evil spoken of, that which belongs to man as possessing an animal nature and that which does not belong to him as of his own humanity, but which enters into him and takes possession of him, that which we call Satanic. It does not seem to me possible to read the New Testament references to evil intelligently, unless we keep this distinction in mind. The Church of Rome has tried to preserve the distinction in the well-known words "mortal and venial sins." It does not seem to me that the terms are well chosen. But the fact that such a distinction in the quality of sins has been made, is instructive and noteworthy. Protestantism has often spoken of sins of infirmity, and sins of will. In the one case a man errs not meaning to err, he sins not meaning to rebel against God. The roots of his sin are in his ignorance, in his non-perception of the nature of certain acts. Some sins are fallen virtues. But other sins have no affinity with virtues. They are of such a nature as to take possession of the inner spirit and dry up the very springs of repentance. In such a case a man's heart never melts into sorrow and his lips never utter the word of contrition. Our humanity when it is Christianized readily recognizes that some sinners are more to be pitied than blamed. Now, from all sins of this class and from the evils they bring, death will come as a rescue. That part of the man in which the inherited tendencies to these sins reside will drop away. The soul enters into new surroundings and conditions. That which injures and tends to kill the body may still leave the soul, if not unstained, yet not separated from God. The man who has never meant to be a God-defier and hater, who has never meant to injure his neighbor, must be of a different quality, whatever his natural infirmities, from the man who has been both a God-defier and a man-hater.

Those who fear not God, nor regard man, are in a condition far more hopeless than many whose sins are more outspoken in their character. Search into our Lord's life, notice how He speaks as he comes into contact with different types of sinners, how pitiful he is towards one class, how full of insuppressible indignation in the presence of others, a holy defiance trembles in His tones — what is the meaning of this destinction? In the one case he meets sin which is almost all infirmity, in the other case sin, calling itself virtue, whose core is unrepenting malignity. In the one case he is the physician to human helplessness, in the other case he confronts that kingdom whose darkness enters into the very spirit of man destroying faith and hope. In the one case he touches the sin which belongs to fallen humanity, in the other he finds men in league with the Evil One, acting like children of the devil, and he came to destroy the works of the devil and to give man his deliverance from the devil power. I think we are justified in the inference that death indicates the time of deliverance from all evils which are not Satanic in their quality. "Fear not them which kill the body, and after that have no more that they can do."

The third idea is — that of a more dreadful enemy than those who kill the body. We are, in this world, occupied chiefly with evils which report themselves in the body. Not everyone recognizes that there may be evils more dire and dreadful than these, whose seat is the soul, deliverance from which would not come with rescue from the conditions which bind us while we are in this material body. There is a Personal Power, says our Lord, which prompts the murderers of the body to do their dire work. That is the dreadful enemy; you cannot regard that enemy with too much dread and horror. It is a power which delights in condemnation and destruction. Its sphere of operation is not confined to this world. It has access here through the worst men and women who are in the world. They are the gateway through which it enters. I know how we all shrink from looking into this region. It is a dark and doleful realm. We seem helpless when called upon to fight an enemy who works in the dark. Even murder has its degrees and assassination is the meanest form of murder. An enemy who gives you no chance of flight or defence is the lowest specimen of an enemy. Now, when social reformers plead with men to forsake their vices, they almost invariably point to results which are of the earth, earthy. They say to the chronic drunkard, look at the social disgrace which you bring upon yourself, the desolateness of your home, the poverty of your children, disease lurking in your blood, and so on. All these are material results and possibly, in most cases, they

are the only results which can be talked about.
But there are subtler and worse results than
these. Supposing the poverty and beggary should
be avoided and the coarser material results
should not press themselves upon the attention, is
there nothing else in the home deplorable, nothing
else in man still more deplorable? Think of a
woman of natural nobleness of soul, with delicate
refinement of taste, and educated mind, whose
chief pleasures would be in the mental and affectional regions, bound hand and foot to a man who
is a chronic drunkard, and then conceive, if you
can, of the unspoken misery of such a state. It
is not the misery of wanting bread, or the misery
of "looped and windowed raggedness," but a far
deeper misery than that. Then think again of the
meanness of soul which comes to the man himself,
of the loss of all nobleness and all real refinement
and consideration for others; *these*, the moral and
spiritual results, are far worse than the material.
We begin to touch that region which our Lord
opens to us when the soul becomes the prey of a
malignant power from which it cannot rescue
itself. Not that this is by any means the only or
chief gateway through which that malignant power
gets access to the soul; I quote it only to show
that there are worse evils than the material to
which social reformers point.

These I have named are the dire facts of life;

there is no fancy here; no invention; no speculation; we are face to face with facts, enemies who kill the body, men of the slaughter-house, but after that have no more that they can do; and revealed to us more fully by Jesus the Christ than it was ever revealed before, a power whose aim is to destroy both body and soul, a malignant power, the whole of whose nature and history we shall never know in this world. But notice now, I beg of you, what follows; notice what is the next word which falls from our Lord's lips. He anticipates the dismay which will come to human hearts as he utters these words about the men who kill the body and the more malignant power which aims to destroy the soul. He sees the hopeless look. He hears the groan of the sympathetic heart. He notes the question shaping itself into form. Alas, what is a man to do in such a world and in presence of such powers of evil? And so, immediately, with a haste that seems like an abrupt transition from one subject to another, He asks, "Are not five sparrows sold for two farthings, and not one of them is forgotten in the sight of God. But the very hairs of your head are all numbered. Fear not, ye are of more value than many sparrows." He meets all the fear and apprehension of the soul in presence of these appalling facts by a declaration of the minuteness and universality of the Divine Providence. Where is the protection from this malignant power of evil?

Utter, absolute trust in God — that is the refuge from the evil and destroying spirit. In the presence of great destructive forces you feel your own insignificance. But you are not more insignificant than the birds, are you? God cares for them. You cannot deliver yourself from these destructive powers, but God can deliver you from them. That is the connection between one thought and the other. The Providence of God is so deep, so broad, that it can allow to men and devils a freedom which seems appalling, and yet it can put up insurmountable barriers beyond which these evil powers cannot go. That is our Lord's teaching. And it is teaching that every mind needs, specially minds that are imaginative, brooding, thoughtful, contemplative, otherwise these minds will relapse into darkness, into unbelief, into godlessness. Poor Cowper (the poet) mused and mused and mused till he went mad, but he recovered himself and wrote: —

> God moves in a mysterious way
> His wonders to perform;
> He plants his footsteps in the deep
> And rides upon the storm.
>
> Blind Unbelief is sure to err,
> And scan his work in vain;
> God is His own interpreter,
> And He will make it plain.

XIV.

FOR HIS NAME'S SAKE.

I write unto you, little children, because your sins are forgiven you for His name's sake.—1 *John*, ii: 12.

THIS language of St. John is somewhat hazy. A kind of mist hangs around it as around a landscape when the all but imperceptible golden veil of an Indian summer is thrown over it. Some land is naturally so rich that it throws up its veil of modest mist and then when the Sun permeates it, everywhere is a whisper of color, but it is color which *reveals* not conceals, like the color on the peach which reveals that it is luscious to the very centre. And so the mind of St. John throws off its own enriching atmosphere, simply because it is itself so rich and mellow through its easy permeableness. The human love of Jesus found a resting place in this disciple's heart, and in that fact is the secret of the sweet mysticism of the Apostle. Each heart throws off its own atmosphere, as each flower its own perfume. In the company of St. Paul men would feel able to do and to dare. In

that of St. John they would feel the deep need of
fellowship, of being in loving sympathy with each
other and with God. Inspiration did not change
each of these men into the other, it used that
which was best in each individual and thus brought
all into sympathetic fellowship with the Christ
of God.

Living in the joy and light of the Divine Fatherhood, the Apostle John had come to regard all disciples of Jesus as children; and as the beauty of a
child is in its childhood, its littleness, its unassert-
iveness, its dependableness, the Apostle seems to
have a delight in speaking of the disciples of Jesus
as little children, remembering doubtless the little
child that Jesus took and set in the midst of those
disciples who were wrangling about greatness and
place and position. These three terms which he
uses — fathers, young men, little children — are not
picked up at random, but chosen deliberately and
with design — " fathers " for knowledge; " young
men " for strength; " little children " because of
their complete dependableness. We must bear
this in mind or we shall perhaps be somewhat
inclined to find fault with the Apostle when he
associates the idea of sinfulness with little children.
Their small naughtinesses do not seem of sufficient
gravity to be called sins. And yet, inherited
sinfulness of disposition is at the root of most
of them. But if we look carefully at the form of

this passage it suggests to our minds not a lament over sins, but a congratulation on the fact of sins forgiven. "I write unto you because your sins are forgiven you for His name's sake." The idea in the passage which attracts us is the association of sin with forgiveness, and specially the association of forgiveness with Jesus Christ.

In this week on which we have entered and which is regarded by the sacerdotal churches as specially a holy week, it does not seem to me that there is anything to prevent the Evangelical Churches from approaching Easter day by the gateway of that sacrifice of Himself which our Lord made. Indeed, there seems to be a kind of incongruity about celebrating the Resurrection unless we first of all dwell upon some of the facts and thoughts which made the Resurrection the great triumphant centre of all life. As we intend, on Sabbath next, to turn our thoughts to the Resurrection of our Lord, would it not be as appropriate for us, as for those who belong to the sacerdotal churches, to make this week a time for meditation on the sacrificial work of our Lord and its relation to our deliverance from sin and its consequences?

He made a sacrifice of Himself, and so, in some real and true sense, His life and death must have been sacrificial. He sacrificed Himself in order that we might have our human life preserved to us, and so in some real and true sense His life and death must have been substitutionary. And as His death had relation to the forgiveness of our sins, in some real and true sense, it must have been expiatory. These three elements, the expiatory, the substitutionary, the sacrificial must have entered into what our Lord was and did. Oftentimes, I know, these facts are stated in a very crude and inadequate way. But that is the fault of the statement not of the fact. There is a deep philosophy in the fact. When a citizen dons the garb of a soldier, and goes out to fight for his country, if he dies, he dies that some one else may *not* die, he sacrifices himself that some one else may live. He does not fight his own private battle. He is a representative. And so Jesus Christ was our representative, and sacrificed Himself for us. Not that this illustration covers the ground. It only helps us to make a little progress towards the place where we can see farther into this death of Jesus. But all our explanations leave much unexplained, for we cannot look into the deeps of sin or the deeps of life, or what is necessary in order to God being just and the justifier of Him who believes in Jesus.

I think however, that there is much of instruction, and no little of comfort for us if only we will try to see things as the Apostle John sees them.

He acknowledges the dark fact of sin, the

bright fact of forgiveness, and the brightest of all facts — that forgiveness is based on the relation which Jesus Christ has established between Himself and us.

Believing that we do not make enough of this brightest of all bright facts, that forgiveness is based on the relation which Jesus the Christ has established between Himself and us, I would ask you specially to fix your attention on this.

Not that I mean to suggest that we make too much of the dark fact of sin. On the contrary we talk about it too much and think about it too little. If we had any deep apprehension of what sin is, we could never jest about it as we do so often. We should feel it to be the radical defect in our nature, so radical that nothing that we could do ourselves, if left to ourselves, could prevent its being fatal. That shallow theology which says "If only a man repent of his sin it is all right" would not find much favor from us. The sin of man is so radical that if left alone he never will repent of it; for he will never see sin as sin. He will see it only as defect,— defect excusable on the ground that to err is human. In old times leprosy was the disease which stood for sin, for the reason that it was an incurable disease. Christ touched the leper to show men that what was incurable with man was curable with God. There was a world of suggestion in that touch of

Christ. There is no possibility of man curing his own sin by his own repentance. Repentance is an effect not a cause. It is the effect of the Spirit of God entering a human spirit and starting a new life in it.

I do not mean to offer any words that are saturated with reproachfulness, but in our most thoughtful moments I think we must, some of us, be surprised at the pitiful poverty of much which passes for thinking on some of these vital themes. One is weary of hearing of secular education as a cure for the radical sinfulness of man's nature. I am sure that an eloquent writer of our day is right on this—that if the influence of the outpoured life of Christ were withdrawn from our world, sins would not only increase incalculably in number, but the tyranny of sin would be fearfully augmented, and it would spread among a greater number of people. Falsehood would become so universal as almost to dissolve society; and the homes of domestic life would be turned into the wards, either of a prison or a mad-house. We can not be in the company of an atrocious criminal without some feeling of uneasiness and fear. We should not like to be left alone with him, even if his chains are not unfastened. Withdraw the outpoured life of Christ from the world and why should not such men be the majority? Some one says, Educate, Educate; Education (of the mind only apart from education of the heart) multiplies and magnifies our powers of sinning. That refinement adds a fresh malignity. Under the power of the education of the intellect only you but sharpen the claws of the lion and whet the fangs of the tiger. Under the power of secular education only men may become more and more diabolically and unmixedly bad, until at last earth would be a hell on this side of the grave. There would doubtless be new kinds of sin and worse kinds. Education would provide the novelty, and refinement would carry it into the region of the unnatural. All highly refined and luxurious developments of heathenism have fearfully illustrated this truth. A wild barbarian is like a beast. His savage passions are violent but intermittent, and his necessities of sin do not appear to grow. Their circle is limited. But a highly-educated sinner, without the restraints of religion, is like a demon. His sins are less confined to himself. They require others to be offered in sacrifice to them.

If only we had read more carefully our histories, the history of Greece, refined linguistically and in regard to Art beyond anything accomplished since; the history of Rome with its legal education, its military discipline, its æsthetic training in oratory and the art of poetry, so that even now Horace and Virgil stand all but peerless in their ranks, we should not too much exalt education so far as it means the sharpening of the intellect. Or, if we went to the Orient, is the *Buddhist* an uneducated man? The subtlest-thoughted people in the world are in the Orient. If you doubt it, ask Emerson. He knew. And yet these educations produced a wide-spread *despair*. And what does that mean? Despair, it means always and everywhere, "rage, madness, violence, tumult, bloodshed." Verily we are saved by hope. But how to get the hope. Hope does not come to men who need it, simply by telling them it is a good thing and brings brightness into the soul. Flowers are good things and bring brightness into our gardens, but they never come except you can pour sunlight, and not frosty sunlight either, into the beds in which the seeds lie slumbering. Christians ought to have reached an order of intelligence which would restrain them from giving their endorsement to that kind of thinking which seems to have something in it because it is so well-dressed. All the classics and mathematics in the world cannot touch the root of the evil which curses man. It is a new disposition, a new heart which man needs, and the outpoured life of God in Christ is necessary to produce that; as necessary to produce it as the outpoured radiance of the Sun is necessary to produce the fruits of the earth by which our physical nature is sustained.

Has not God given us in nature parables illustrative of the great facts of spiritual life? At times God seems to be at a great distance from us, at so great a distance that we can live our life without taking Him and what He can do for us into the account. We even think that it is problematical whether He have any touch upon us or not. We seem to live from earth-born forces and within earth-born conditions. Ought not such musings to be seen in their true nature when we think that we are really dependent upon light and heat generated ninety millions of miles from us, for every violet gathered by a child's hand in the early spring-time, for every blushing rose in June, even for every common potato which comes to our table. If it were not for that great furnace ninety millions of miles off, our globe would be an icicle glittering in the semi-darkened depths of space, a dimly visible gem on the sable bosom of night. There is nothing which lives on the life generated within itself. Man cut off from the outpoured radiance of the Divine Nature would be as the earth cut off from the Sun. The man who curses God, the man whose profanity declares the innate vulgarity of his mind, is obliged to inhale from God's reservoir of life the very breath with which to curse his Maker. In God's Universe the distant and the near are in fellowship, and so, too, in God's spiritual realm, the Redemptive forces which often seem far off, are not really so. "I am with you alway, even to the end of the world," was no mere figure of speech. As the sunlight enters into every flower that blooms and every fruit that ripens, so Christ's life enters into every soul that breathes the prayer, "God be merciful to me a sinner." Therefore it is that the Apostle John goes far deeper than to connect the forgiveness of sin with repentance for sin, he connects it with the relationship we sustain to Christ and the relationship He sustains to us. And if only you will think of it, there is much more of consolation in this fact than in anything we can say about repentance. There is always room for doubt as to the reality and sincerity of our repentance. There is always room to doubt its genuineness, its sufficiency, its quality. Will such repentance as I can give ever satisfy the Divine Holiness? If it will not, what is the good of it? What use to torment myself about it? If I cannot be sure of anything I offer being the genuine and right thing, what comfort can I get out of anything I do? The human mind is sure to reason in this way. If a man builds his house on the sands and there is nothing beneath but sand, he will tremble when the tempest-driven tide thunders in. All our experiences, all our feelings, all our ideas of ourselves are poor, sandy foundations on which to build hopes for Eternity. So long as a man is playing with religion, almost anything that sounds religious will do for him; but once let real thoughtfulness sieze him, once let him look into the depths of his own nature and see "what incredible possibilities of wickedness we have in our souls," *then* nothing but the real thing will do. Henceforth his repentances, his experiences, his feelings, anything and everything belonging to him are regarded as poor foundations on which to build hopes. He asks—is there no reason outside myself why God should forgive my sins? All these changeful inner experiences are treacherous as a quicksand. I want something that is not treacherous, something that remains, something that *man* cannot take away from me, something he has not given me. It is this state of mind to which the Apostle John appeals when he says, "I write unto you little children because your sins are forgiven you for His name's sake." I do not for a single moment assume that I have the vision to look into the profundities of the Divine and Human natures so as to see to the depths of this theme. Some one asks—why is it necessary that Jesus the Christ of God should put Himself into the relations towards us which have been established, in order that the Everlasting Father may forgive sins? Why cannot He say to the sorrowing man "I forgive you," and have done with it? Well, it seems to me there are reasons in His own nature; there are reasons in man's nature; there are reasons in the Divine Government.

There are reasons in His own nature. When God undertakes to *forgive* sin He pledges Himself to rescue the forgiven man from his sin. In a word, He undertakes to regenerate his nature, to renew it so that he shall eventually live the unsinning life. And in order to that, Jesus Christ and His work are necessary.

There are reasons in the nature of man. To forgive a sinner and leave him to the helplessness which has come from his sin is only *half* forgiveness. Man needs to be brought into such an understanding of God and into such a love of God that he will hate to sin against Him. In order to that, Christ Jesus and His sacrifice of Himself are necessary. Mere *words* will not do. There must be some Divine Act which will stand unapproachable, and incapable of being paralleled. Jesus the Christ has supplied that act.

There are reasons too in the Divine Government, but we have not time to state them beyond saying that it must be made universally evident that there is no righteous reason for rebellion against God on the part of any. This we may be sure of — that in its most serious moments, when thought surges within like a sea lashed with tempest, the heart of man must have from God something more than mere *words* to still the storm. On Galilee's lake there is a boat's crew battling with tempest. *They can do nothing with the winds and waves.* The gusty howl of the wind, the frothy fury of the waves, blanch their cheeks and still their tongues. But, walking on the wave, One comes with a quietude which is itself sublime, and there is a great calm. Not for nothing was that scene given us. The tumult that rages within this human life of ours seems endless. Nothing abates it. Every age has its controversies. Every life has its storms. The moan of the sorrowful and the distressed, the whine of the restless and dissatisfied, the demoniac howl of the bad, are all heard — heard by every generation. Only the miraculously frivolous and the supernaturally stoical do not hear them. Mere words will not allay our fears or excite our hopes. We need a man who is more than man to come and walk on these waves and say to us, "That which is impossible with man is possible with God." And so Jesus comes. He comes to us to be one of us. He comes and steps into the boat. He says, "If you perish I will perish with you." He comes to put Himself at our head. He comes and takes on Himself the responsibility for our being born with sinful tendencies. He says — Let the sin do its worst on *me*. I will be the guilty one, by identifying myself with the guilty. If sin has any rights let it take them out of me. If it has a right to kill, let it kill *me. Then*, I will bring all the forces of my Immortal Being into operation to rescue men from it. As David stood for all Israel in presence of Goliath, I will stand for all humanity. Single-handed I will fight its battles. The Goliath of Sin shall fall before me. And then I will demand forgiveness of sin for all who are willing to take it at my hands. And so it is. As was said to Paul in the ship, ' God hath given thee all who sail with thee,' so to Jesus Christ it can be said, God hath given thee all for whom thou didst die. Hence, "He is the Savior of all men, specially of those who believe." Hence St. John's congratulatory words, "I write unto you, little children, because your sins are forgiven you," inasmuch as ye have repented enough? No, no. Inasmuch as ye have had correct spiritual experiences? No, no. Inasmuch as ye are strictly orthodox in all points of theology? No, no. Inasmuch as there is a strong probability that you will be found worthy to receive the Divine endorsement at the last? No, no—"I write unto you, my little children, *because your sins are forgiven you for His name's sake.*"

I am glad St. John wrote these words rather than any of the other Apostles, because he it was who stood it out beneath the Cross and saw what sin could do. He saw it erect that Cross. He heard its vulgar reproach, its mockery, its words of scorn, and though his heart must have been nigh to breaking, he endured it. Brave, good, gentle soul, the King of his heart was there, on that Cross, crowned with thorns it is true, with thorns which "the unsuspecting earth had grown for its Creator. They had grown up into matted bushes, and the sun of autumn had hardened their soft spikes into tough barbs. Perhaps the honey bees had come to these flowers to extract sweetness, and the restless butterflies had been attracted for a moment by their aromatic fragrance, or the birds had rifled their golden berries with their beaks," but when the sun, that had hardened their soft spikes into tough barbs, saw that to such uses they were put, the very sun hid his face in despair, and there was darkness over all the land from the sixth to the ninth hour. Crowned with thorns, but yet the King of all human hearts, as John felt. Glad am I that it was John, the disciple whom Jesus loved, the disciple whose love never failed, even when his faith received the rudest shock; the disciple who saw what sin could do, who wrote these words, "your sins are forgiven you, for His name's sake."

And so we are delivered from the harassing questions as to the sincerity, the genuineness, the sufficiency of our repentance. Repentance has its place, not an obscure one, in Christian experience. But, I repeat, it is an effect not a cause. If only we can read these words with that understanding of them which comes from the possession of a Christianized heart, they will be far more satisfactory to us than any other; "Your sins are forgiven you for His name's sake." The first moment after death is a moment which must infallibly come to every one of us. Earth lies behind us silently wheeling its obedient way through the black-tented space. Will it make no difference then, as the measureless Eternity stretches before us, and the thought of a life which will seem a failure lies behind, that these words have been sent us by the lips of him who knew how to love but not how to desert the One he so much loved, "your sins are forgiven you for His name's sake."

XV.

SEARCHINGS OF HEART.

"Behold and see if there be any sorrow like unto my sorrow."—*Lamentations of Jeremiah*, i: 12.

THE greatest natures are capable of the greatest sorrow. It is utterly inconceivable to man of how much sorrow a nature like that of Jesus is capable. The prophet saw Him in vision, and His visage was more marred than that of any man's. What sorrow would be ours if, for a single day, we were endowed with a power of vision which enabled us to see underneath all the coverings of life, into the heart of things; if all persons were laid bare to us, and we saw the stern reality below the veneer and polish and dress and shows of things! Yet the Divine Eye traverses that region, and none can cover up the interior life from His burning gaze. Is the Divine heart impassive and unmoved by what it sees? Has it no suffering on account of it?

There are two kinds of suffering, two kinds of sorrow. There is the suffering and sorrow of guilt — dry, hard, and without contrition; there is also the suffering and sorrow of love, which faintly represents the inner movements of the Divine heart. We cannot say what compensations of joy are in the Divine Nature, but that it is an impassive nature, *that* we cannot believe so long as we hold by Scripture. To no one so thoroughly as to a Divine Being has this question such broad and deep application — "Behold and see if there be any sorrow like unto my sorrow."

Let us dwell for a short while on this thought. Let us not forget that the sufferings of our Lord historically recorded, are but part of His sufferings. To the Colossians the great Apostle speaks of "filling up that which is behind of the afflictions of Christ." There are sorrows for the Son of man still, for he has identified Himself with us, and become one with us. To Paul, afflictions and trials were radiant with a golden light of privilege, because, more than ought else they brought him into such close fellowship with the great Sufferer.

And does not our Lord suffer *now?* Does not His *church* cause Him sorrow? Is it not like raw material, so very hard to his hand as to be almost incapable of being moulded into any shape or form of beauty? Does He not sorrow over our ignorance? Our mental dullness? Our pride of knowledge which is often worse than ignorance? Our assumptions of something so like infallibility that no one can distinguish it from the real thing itself? Our unteachablenes? Our cantankerousness? Our unloveliness of spirit and unloveableness? Our hard thoughts of others? Our want of charity towards them that see not with us, eye to eye, in opinion? Do not these things cause Him sorrow?

Again, our want of patience in doing His work? Our expecting to reap on the very day we sow? Our pettishness and peevishness with one another; our ill-humor, which gives a diseased color to our eye so that everything seems to have a jaundiced and fading look; everything seems to be "in the sere and yellow leaf," and we find no cause of thankfulness to God anywhere. Does He not sorrow over our suspicion, that spirit which is the opposite of the charity which thinketh no evil, the spirit which sees nothing in those who are not with us but whited sepulchres and platters clean but on the outside? Does He not sorrow over our self-importance, that spirit which leads us to suppose that *we* must always be right and *others* always wrong; that we are called to sit on thrones not only to judge the erring and wandering twelve tribes of Israel, but the tribes of the spiritual Israel also.

Does not our Lord sorrow over our legalism — that old Jewish spirit of slavishness to mere forms and customs which are of human device—the letter which killeth; the rigidity which knows not how to bend or adapt itself to weakness and feebleness and infirmity?

Must He not sorrow over our sectarianisms — our thinking more of mere sectional names than of the real unity which underlies all these? Must He not sorrow over that mental and spiritual obtuseness which cannot, or will not, see that a man may be a very rigid sectarian and a very bad Christian; that he may be most scrupulously excellent at such work as "tithing mint, anise, and cummin," but for the weightier matters of justice, judgment, and truth he may have no very sincere appreciation? Must He not sorrow over our injudicious, oftentimes almost untruthful speech; over that very great freedom that we allow ourselves, even in the presence of young children, to criticise, severely and unkindly, our fellow-members, our deacons, our ministers? The tongue is a fire, a world of iniquity, says the Apostle James. And he calls the man who has perfect control over his speech a perfect man. "In many things we all offend; if any man offend not in word the same is a perfect man, and able also to bridle the whole body." Must not our hard speech, speech destitute of love and feeling and tender consideration for others, be a cause of sorrow to our Divine Lord?

Yea — sometimes, must not our very *prayers* be

a source of sorrow to Him? "Ye ask and receive not, because ye ask amiss, that ye may consume it on your lusts." Have we had no lust at the root of our desire? No lust of power? No lust of influence? No lust of lording it over others? No lust of impressing our own peculiar individualism on others? Have we longed to see the poor crowding into our church courts? Have we not secretly prayed that this and that person of influence might be brought in? But have we felt glad — rejoiced — when some poor servant girl has come? *Have* we? Have we thought that all our prayers and anxieties were more than answered by such a result as that?

If there had been but that *one* soul lost, still Redemption's work must all have been given for that one soul. Have our prayers been winged by Lazarus at the gate, or by Dives in the palace? Must not our Lord have had sorrow oftentimes over our limiting the Holy One of Israel; over our very defective appreciation of the diversity of His operations? Have we not dug out our channels, and laid our waterpipes and connected them with some favorite reservoir of opinion, and said within ourselves, "Come, O Spirit of Grace, into *these* — or, I can have no delight in thee?" But, instead of that, oftentimes the influences have not come down our channels. They have been dry. Yet in other ways God has sent His blessing, have we delighted in it? Have we not too often had that Naaman-spirit, which was not humble enough to receive a blessing just in the way which God had designed it should come, "Surely, I thought," has been our reply. And then, has not some weak and gentle voice whispered in our ear, "If the prophet had bid thee do some *great* thing, wouldst thou not have done it? Have we never been proudly ambitious to do some great thing? Have we never sought *reputation* simply and been heedless of *character?* And has not our Lord had continual sorrow because of this?

Have we not been, like Peter, sometimes impertinently officious about others, instead of careful about our own spirits? "Lord and what shall this man do?" Have we not *forced* our Lord to be sharp with us?—"If I will that he tarry till I come, what is that to thee; follow thou me?"

Instead of simply being *disciples*, and cherishing the spirit of disciples, have we never done anything, or said anything to convey to others the impression that we are models of Christian attainment, paragons of excellency, just what others ought to be, in short, the guardians and watch-dogs of the church, licensed by our very nature to snap and bark at all intruders, or, like Scotch sheep-dogs, trained to worry the sheep into the fold? Have none of us given just cause for men to say, ' if it were not for such hard men as that man, and that man, such unlovable men, I should think better of Christians?' Dear brethren, are we free from that spiritual Pharisaism, that ill-natured spiritual conceit which repels, from which even contrite souls recoil? Often, very often, no one but God knows how often, I have to compel my own spirit just to take its proper position, that of a sinner at the foot of the Cross. I dare not approach God as a saint. I believe that I know something of what the Apostle felt when he wrote, "less than the least of all saints." Are we Christian brethren, content to be simply disciples of Jesus, sinners saved by grace, to stand where Paul chose to stand, a position dignified enough surely for any man, not boasting ourselves of how much we love Christ, but rejoicing in this, that He loved us, "who loved me, and gave Himself for me?"

Yes, truly, our Lord may well say, as He looks into the hearts of the members of His professing Church, "Behold and see, if there be any sorrow like unto my sorrow." When, in a court of Justice, a man's own witnesses seem to damage his cause, the case is indeed pitiful.

And yet, our Lord's deepest, profoundest, tenderest sorrow does not arise from any inconsistencies, or defects, or blunders, or ignorances, or wilfulnesses which He sees among those who believe in Him, trust Him and look to Him, many of whom do their feeble, blundering best, to serve Him. For, every man who names the name of Christ, and departs from iniquity, honors Christ. Just as every young man who enters a school honors that school, by the trust he reposes in its teachers. Just as a tyro in art honors a great Master by copying his works. Christ's church is practically a school; not a museum in which to deposit specimens of antique theologies and dead saints; not a gallery of painting and sculpture in which to display finished productions; it is a school for Christians in the making. There are no finished specimens to be found in it. This world is God's manufactory, not His show-room. But wherever there is trust in God and confidence towards God, there is reconciliation with God. There is no Christian man without his inconsistencies, but these are the mere unfinished parts of character. And yet, between the soul that trusts itself into Christ's hands, and the soul that witholds itself for itself, there is a whole gulf of difference. Naturally, one may be a finer specimen of man than the other, intellectually superior, more refined in sensibility, more companionable, and yet as to the interior possibilities there is no comparison. Christ in a man, as Paul puts it, may be but as a seed in him, but it is a seed which shall rend the rock, and split the mountain in its growth. Christ in a man is a germ in Him which demands Eternity for its development. Therefore is it that to get the idea of Christ uppermost in the mind renews the mind, to get the love of Christ supreme in the heart renews the affectional nature. As to those who trust Him, our Lord can wait the perfect development of Himself into dominion over all weaknesses, ignorances, wilfulnesses, inconsistencies whatsoever. It is a mere matter of time. His chief sorrow is from another source. His chief sorrow was not over Peter who denied Him; not over the two disciples who wanted to be the greatest in His kingdom; not over Magdalene whose soul He cleansed of its seven-fold tyranny of evil—for she loved much, having much forgiven— not over Nicodemus who came secretly, under the deep shadows of night; not over the disciples who slept in Gethsemane and could not watch with Him one hour; not over the men who forsook Him and fled; not even over the dying thief. His chief sorrow was not over these, but over the people of the city who rejected Him—"Oh, Jerusalem, Jerusalem, thou that killest the prophets, and stonest them which are sent unto thee, how often would I have gathered thy children together, even as a hen gathereth her chickens under her wings, and ye would not!"—over Judas who betrayed Him, "good for that man had he never been born." And, in these days, His chief sorrow is not over His Church, with all its multiplied inconsistencies, ignorances, and wilfulnesses, but over others; over you young man, to whom He has given a godly father and mother, who daily pray for you, though you hear it not, who love you with a love that as far as a finite thing can represent an infinite thing, is like the love of God. Oh, to be born in Heaven and to descend into Hell; to be cradled in Bethlehem and thence to sink into an inhabitant of Sodom; to breathe your first breath in the land of Promise, and to choose in preference the bondage of Egypt; to resist successfully the undying solicitude of a heart beating with a pulse that is timed to God's love; to be the child of a house on the lintel and side-posts of which the blood of Calvary had been sprinkled; to be dedicated to God in Baptism; to have all the privileges of the Kingdom of Heaven claimed on your behalf; to be a child of God's Covenant made with your parents, and to break away, finally and forever from this, it seems to me at times impossible. It seems to me at times as if the *power* of God as well as the *grace* of God were pledged to your arrestment. Our Lord looking on you may well say, "was any sorrow, like unto my sorrow?"

Over you also, fathers and mothers, men and women bearing the holiest names that this world knows; into whose arms a gift has been placed than which this earth can furnish none so marvellous or wonderful — have you appreciated that gift at its true value? Have you realized that the flesh was only a platform for an immortal spirit to stand upon? Must there not be sorrow in the heart of Christ as He sees fathers and mothers treating children as though they were mere animal forms, or at the most, mere children of this world, to be trained for this world, everything nurtured in them *except* that which is highest, that which is distinctive, that which makes them men? In every child there is a religious instinct, and it largely depends upon what the parents are as to whether that religious instinct shall be cultured or crushed; whether it shall become *conviction*, or remain for a while in an undeveloped condition and eventually become an accusing Conscience. I believe that most of the sad disappointments that parents meet with in their children are simply Nature working its own revenge for this insult offered to the religious instinct. Have those of you who are fathers and mothers not brought much sorrow into the heart of Jesus by refusing to train the religious instinct in your child? That which fathers and mothers do, children naturally want to do. Are you, fathers and mothers, just exactly where you ought to be, considering what your opportunities and responsibilities are? You love your children, why do you not love them *all through*, soul as well as body, spirit as well as soul? I have sometimes met with cases of parents who said to their children, "go," but not "come." Better, far better life than speech. Better example than precept. But more human and kindly the spirit which says, "go" than that which *resists* the religious instinct of childhood in its feelings after God. What must have been the sensations of that mother, whose son, in the condemned cell, turned upon her, almost with the rage of a tiger, and said, "If you had been a better woman I should never have been here."

When our Lord looks from the height of His Infinite Knowledge upon the world of fathers and mothers, and sees how, by their example, they are bending their children's souls away from Him, how often must His feeling be like to that expressed in these words, " Is any sorrow like unto my sorrow."

But we cannot pursue this line of reflection into many of its details. And yet does it not touch every one of us? What sorrow greater than that of being perpetually misunderstood? And who knows this sorrow as the Son of God knows it? Have we not misunderstood Him most egregiously? Have we not thought of Him as the condemner? Yet is He the Saviour. Have we not regarded Him as though He came to destroy? Yet He came to stand between us and destruction. What sorrow is more cutting and lacerating and torturing to the heart than to be suspected? Has not Jesus been the object of our suspicion? Have we not said by our conduct, 'I dare not trust Him, I dare not commit myself to Him?' Have we not exalted men above Him? Have we not feared men? Have we not allowed the frowns of men to be more to us than the smiles of the Savior? Have we not steadily refused to follow our best inclinations? Have we not done our best to put out the light which was in our consciences? Have we not resisted our own tenderest impulses? Have we not thought that we might have too much of Christ? Have we not persisted in thinking that the call of Christ was to gloom, and despondency and joylessness and narrowness of life? Have we not ignorantly misinterpreted the plainest truths of Holy Writ? Have we not resisted the Holy Spirit's movements in our souls? Have we not almost forced ourselves into darkness? And all this has been so much of *sorrow* poured into the lot of the Son of Man. Yet still He broods over us, with a love that many waters cannot quench. Still He shows us His Crown of Thorns, His garments all red with blood, His pierced hands and feet, His spear thrust side; still He reminds us of Calvary, and of Gethsemane and asks us still, "Was any sorrow like unto my sorrow?"

XVI.

THE DIVINE RESPONSIBILITY.

But now thus saith the Lord that created thee, O Jacob, and He that formed thee, O Israel, Fear not, for I have redeemed thee, I I have called thee by thy name: thou are mine.—*Isaiah*, xliii: 1.

THE subject of Responsibility has recently occupied our attention. First, the Responsibility of the Ungodly for his ungodliness and all its consequences. Secondly, the Responsibility of the Christian — consisting mainly in loyalty to Christ. And now I am about to venture upon an extension of this thought of Responsibility. I purpose to pursue it into a region, the most sacred of all — and to speak — I hope without presumption, I hope with reverence, I hope so as not to expose myself to any just charge of rashness or impiety — I propose to speak of the Divine responsibility.

For, surely, Responsibility is not a word that can be limited to man. It must belong to those higher orders of created intelligence known to us as angels of various degrees. It must belong to the Eternal One Himself. It must be that He holds Himself *responsible* for the Creation and its consequences. This is not a thought that often comes within the sphere of our meditation — nor should it. Such a thought is not to be brought into the area of flippant discussion or heated controversy. It belongs rather to those moments of meditation when all voices are quiet but one, and that one voice chastened into subduedness consistent with the deepest reverence. And yet surely we may speak on so sacred a theme without being blameworthy. If responsibility belongs to the creature made in the image of God, it is inherited responsibility; it comes down from Him who made him.

Let us approach the subject cautiously. God's revelation of Himself is intended to be a light to the mind, and a joy to the heart. If the word 'God' means "the good one," be sure that all that is made known to us of God in any way, or through any medium, is for our good. Every word by which He has made Himself known is our property — to be sacredly guarded for what it contains. Everyone who knows anything of Scripture knows how gradual has been the revelation of God to the human race. Not till we reach the time of David do we get the word *father* as applied to Deity, and then only in a figurative sort of way. Isaiah prophecies that one of the signs of the Christian dispensation shall be that the name of God as revealed in Christ shall be "the Everlasting Father." Men had known Deity as the Self-Existent God—the source of life. They had thought of Him as the God of Providence, the Great Provider, who had them in His hands, and would care for them, and that is about the utmost practical view attained in the Old Testament. In that wonderful book of Job, the epitomised life of the human race, we have the thought of an unrealized Redeemer,—but "My Father and your Father, my God and your God" is New Testament language, and post-resurrection speech at that. This speech leads us to the thought of the Divine Responsibility. It is not our invention but God's revelation, that, 'like as a father pitieth his children so the Lord pitieth them that fear Him.' We have a right, then, to say that at least the same measure of responsibility which belongs to a father for the nourishment, education, and development of his child belongs to the great Eternal Father for us all. He has made us, and not we ourselves. We are not responsible for being here—that responsibility belongs outside of us. We are not responsible for the laws which work in our own constitutions, for we did not create those laws. We are not responsible for anything which is out of our own power, that is evident—so evident that it is useless to argue the matter. I am not responsible for the original tendency to sinfulness which was in my nature when born into this world. Nor am I responsible for being born, nor for being born where I was born; nor for having just those parents which were mine; nor for being just so high and just so heavy; nor for having the temperament and disposition with which I was born. Nor are you responsible for like matters in yourself; nor is any one. These things lie beyond our election and choice. Neither you, nor I, nor any one is responsible for the fact that we came into the world puling babes, nor for the laws at the back of our life which co-operated to that result — all this responsibility lies outside of us. I suppose that in the generations behind us there have lived people who verily persuaded themselves that they were responsible for the sin of Adam — that the guilt of what was done thousands of years ago rested upon them — that they were doomed because an ancestor of generations ago was a wilful sinner.

It is very wonderful that any one should be found capable of training his conscience to the acceptance of such a fallacy. Every man inherits tendencies from past generations — that we know. When the first of men wilfully disobeyed God, He started in himself a tendency, which, if not resisted, would become a habit of wrong doing — and that habit would create a tendency in the next generation, and in the next, and so on. And that is what is meant by original sin — the tendency created by generations past to wrong — stamping its impress upon mind and heart, yea, upon the physical organism. It is so in the animal world. In the past, dogs have been trained to fold sheep, and the instruction has become a habit, and the habit has created a tendency in the next generation to do the same thing, and has become fixed — a second nature, as we say. And this law runs through all creation, even into the vegetable world. Drunkenness in a parent creates a tendency to drunkenness in a child. The thieving propensity in a family has been known to propagate itself from generation to generation. The disposition to speak falsehood, too — until whole nations have lost the sense of the deep disgrace of lying. Now, this is what theology means by original sin. It has no idea of original *guilt*. It is contradiction in language, and confusion in thought to speak of original guilt.

Now He who made man is responsible for the original law by which tendencies to good and evil can be propagated from sire to son. The law is not evil; it is good. But good laws are often used for bad purposes. An illustration may make it clear. From a reservoir of pure water, pipes are laid to every house in a city. Those pipes were laid for the conveyance of pure, wholesome water for the benefit of a large population. That was the original design and intention. But suppose that city should be besieged by a barbarian army—suppose the army should surround the reservoir and poison the waters, the very pipes which were laid for the conveyance of life would be conduits for the conveyance of death. But that was not their original design. The city which constructed, at a great cost, that water-system, is not responsible for this diabolic abuse of the system. And so our guilt does not extend to Deity. He is responsible for the beneficent law, not for the sin which has been transmitted along it. The very idea of intelligence involves freedom. Either there must be freedom, or there can be no intelligence and no morality. Man could not be what he is without this liberty. He must have the ability to go wrong, or he cannot have the ability to do right. God is responsible for making man what he is, or rather was, and man is responsible for abusing his freedom. The law is good if a man use it lawfully.

Let us go a step further. We cannot conceive of an Omniscient God, without admitting that He must have foreseen that the creature He made would abuse his liberty. God must have foreseen the fall of His creature from a condition of innocence. Does the Divine Responsibility extend to making such provision as would prevent it?

Clearly not. No such provision has been made. We cannot conceive how it could be made, and yet leave man a free moral agent, not a machine. The Divine responsibility extends to the providing a means whereby not simply to develop an innocent man, but to save a guilty man from the spiritual consequences of his sin. From *all* the consequences he cannot be saved — from the fatal consequences he can. That God did anticipate the fall from innocence of His creature, and provide for meeting man in a fallen condition is evident from one single expression " The Lamb slain before the foundation of the world." In the Divine purpose, plan, and intention, provision was made for the sinner's escape from the fatal consequences of his sin before there was a sinner to sin. Redemption was no after-thought. It was woven into the very web of creation. It was no patching up of badly-done work, as some have irreverently phrased it, but the provision made by Divine Love for all contingencies which should arise. Once apprehend the Divine character as revealed in Holy Writ, and then it will be easy to see that Redemption is the bringing into operation of the Divine Love just as creation is the bringing into operation of the Divine energy. If the Creator puts on this earth a creature with a liability in his nature to fall, is He not responsible for making provision for his redemption and restoration? If you think for a while of the question you will be disposed to give but one answer. I know how often it has been said that if after the fall God had left man to himself, and visited him no more, he would have been just. No one, it is said, could possibly have impeached his justice. It may be so. I do not care to argue the question. I think Scripture does not naturally produce the impression upon the mind that the attributes of God are at variance one with the other, and that there is eternal discord in the Divine nature. It has never produced that impression on my own mind, and I very much question if ever it can be charged with producing that impression on any mind. I have read a discourse in which, with fine dramatic effect, the revealed attributes of Deity were arraigned the one against the other. Justice came with flaming sword, and demanded the execution of the offender. She summoned her witnesses to show that she had done this and that, and sentence was about to be pronounced. But Mercy stepped in and pleaded, with sobs in her voice and tears in her eyes, and at last succeeded in prevailing on Justice to forego her claim. And so for the sake of Mercy — or by Mercy — Justice was defeated. Now, for our own convenience, it may be necessary at times to speak of justice and at other times of mercy. But justice and mercy in God are never represented as in antagonism. They ever go hand-in-hand together — like light and heat in the sunbeams. It would be nothing short of foolish for me to try, in a brief sermon, to offer anything upon what has been called "the philosophy of the plan of salvation." Whether any single human soul has ever been brought into fellowship with Christ through the comprehension of "the philosophy of the plan of salvation," I very much doubt. That part of human nature which we call the 'heart' has more to do with the realizing of the Redemption wrought out on Calvary. The work of Redemption excites a confidence towards God which the work of Creation never can. When the revelation comes to the sinning soul — "Trust in Me; hope in Me; lean upon Me; I have found a Ransom; I am a Just God and a Savior" — a just God, because a Savior — how can such a message do aught else than excite confidence in the soul, and rouse faith into action? We see, from the fact brought into full visibility on Calvary, that the Creator of man holds Himself responsible for man's redemption — that is to say, for doing all and everything essential so to counteract the effects of inherited sin as that it shall be easier for man to reach heaven than not to reach it.

When God opened the eyes of the great apostle he saw this truth, that "Where sin abounded, grace did much more abound," or, as it is more correctly, "superabounded," abounded over and above. In this dispensation of things a lost man has not simply to reject God as a Creator, but God as a Redeemer — God in Christ — the God who has done all and everything possible to be done to nullify the fatal results of sin. There are physical consequences of sin — and these cannot be interfered with. They become useful as chastisements, as evangelical forces in the body of man working a knowledge of what sin is, and under God working repentance for sin. But the *fatal* consequences God has provided against in redemption, for, like as with Paul's ship which was utterly lost, but they who were in it all came safe to land, so with this body of ours, sin-cursed, and therefore not fitted for the permanent body in which the soul shall live eternally; it shall be lost, but the soul shall reach the home-land, and be clothed upon with its house "which is from heaven." In Redemption our God comes to us and shares our responsibility for sin. Oh, it is a wonderful thought that, but a true one! To a degree God makes himself responsible for human sin, and provides redemption, provides a new attitude for the soul. Formerly the law was, Do this and live. Man fell out from that. Now the law is, Trust and live. Have faith and live. "I have found a ransom." As though God should say, the responsibility for sin is not all yours, some of it is Mine. Don't shrink back from the thought. It does not make our

God the author of sin. But He became sin for us who knew no sin. He became as though He were a sinner. In other words, He took upon Himself the responsibility for man's sin to the extent of providing a redemption. And was it not like Him? Think of a father who should blot out the name of his son from the family register the moment he sinned, and do nothing to reclaim him! What would you think of such a father? Would you not go to him and reason with him — "You were the medium of that child's life, he is your child, you are responsible for his existence, and for doing to the utmost possible for that child's redemption and restoration?" And can that which is true of an earthly father towards his child be untrue of the Eternal Father? Having created our spirit's life; having breathed into our nostrils the breath of life, and made us living souls, is the Eternal Father not responsible for the doing all that is possible for Him to do to save us if we sin, to rescue us if we fall, to educate us, to discipline us, and that with all patience, with all tenderness, yet with all the firmness and unyielding righteousness which belong to the fatherly relationship? And herein, in this earthly relationship of father and child, and the responsibility which holds from the one to the other, we get the best commentary the earth holds on the Divine Responsibility.

You remember the complimentary word uttered respecting Abraham: "For I know him that he will command his children;" and in every father there is lodged the right to command — the duty to command. That weak tenderness which permits disobedience to go unrebuked and unpunished, is not Divine tenderness. It is the frailty of human irresoluteness. There is nothing of that in God. The commands and precepts of His Word indicate not merely the magistrate or the ruler. They betoken the Father — the Divine Father — who knows what His children do not know, who would shield them from every harm, and when they are broken and bruised, heal them. Christian brethren, is there nothing for our souls to rest upon in this, that we are not our own creators, not our own in any sense, but God's; that He having created us, is responsible for redeeming us? Does it not help us to get rid of those crude, almost barbaric, thoughts of God, which even Christian minds have sometimes permitted themselves to entertain? Shylock, determined to have his pound of flesh, is not the Bible idea of God. But the Parable of the Prodigal Son is our Lord's idea; and oh, how lovely and beautiful the idea is! Let us cherish it, in the full assurance that it represents — though faintly, yet truly — the eternal disposition of our God towards all returning prodigals and all sorrowing sinners.

XVII.

PREDESTINATION.

"Predestinated according to the purpose of him who worketh all things after the counsel of his own will."— *Ephesians*, i. 11.

HOW often people get frightened at a word. There has been no inconsiderable fright at the first word in this text — 'predestinated' — or, as in the New Version 'fore-ordained.' Calvinism has been associated with such words as 'predestination' and 'fore-ordination.' And these words have been interpreted theologically rather than etymologically. It is very interesting to know what Calvin meant by those words, because he was one of the ruling minds of his time. It is of more importance to know what Paul meant by them — for he was specially called of God to teach spiritual truth because he was specially fitted to teach it — although he did not think that he was. Like Moses, he had a very low idea of his own competency; but the lives of both men proved that there was no mistake made when the one was called to Leadership and the other to Apostleship. The self-distrusting man is generally the man to choose. His distrust of himself will throw him back upon God. "Lord what wilt thou have me to do" will be his perpetual prayer.

What is our relation to leaders in the Church of Christ, leaders of thought, I mean? Tamely to submit to everything they suggest, as though it *must* be truth? Is that our duty?

Or, to resist them simply because they are leaders, in a spirit of snappish independence? Neither the one nor the other. Calvin must have learnt all that he knew of theology from the Apostle Paul. Did he interpret him aright? That is the question. How are we to answer it? By comparing one part of the Apostle's teaching with another — and then comparing the whole of it with what other Apostles said, and specially with what our Lord Himself said and did. Only thus can we know.

Every generation has its way of looking at things. The generation of Calvin saw that there were law and order in the world — and dreaded anarchy, dreaded the uprising of the people, dreaded revolution. They preached a theology of law and order. God was King, absolute monarch, Judge. There was no appeal from Him. So far they were right. But when they went farther and said, we understand perfectly what God's will is, and there is no appeal from *us*, then they went a step too far. Still, the result of their influence on their own time was very beneficial. Never in the world's history, has a city been better ruled than was Geneva under Calvin. And while his interpretations of Scripture have been improved upon in many particulars, yet there are elements in his teaching which are true for ever. Rightly interpreted, the doctrine of the Divine Sovereignty is full of consolation. The inference from it is law and order. If God be not Sovereign who is? Man? But man is a myriad-headed creature. The Sovereignty of man means anarchy. And what shall we say to Calvin's assertion that whatever God wills is right? Read in the light of Scripture it can only mean whatever God wills is good, not simply because He wills it, but because it is for the highest good of His creatures. You may turn the sentence round and read it the other way — whatever is right God wills. Calvin, I have no doubt, felt at heart when he proclaimed the Divine Sovereignty as absolute, and the Divine will as supreme, as felt David when he prayed "Let me fall into the hands of God for His mercies are great, but let me not fall into the hands of man." But whatever Calvin meant, and whatever any great teachers mean, you and I have the same living spring from which to draw our water of life as they had. We can go to the Scriptures themselves. And the only way to arrive at that union of the church of Christ which is so necessary is to go back to the Scriptures. Any man and every man who makes more of mere sectarian leaders than of the leaders which God Himself appointed is condemned by these Scriptures. Read what St. Paul says about this derisive spirit—" One says I am of Paul, another, I am of Apollos, another, I am of Cephas." St. Paul condemns the whole thing. He says, ' while you talk in that way you are carnal in mind, not spiritual. Who is Paul and who is Apollos? Ministers by whom ye believed. Believed in whom? In Paul? In Apollos? Nay; in Christ. It was Christ who was crucified for you. Not Paul, or Apollos or Cephas.' Now this is the spirit which every true successor of the Apostles will stand for. A leader who leads men to himself and not to Christ is a usurper. None of us ought to be satisfied until we are sure that we have correctly apprehended the ideas which these Apostolic men gave to the world. Of course, the man who gives more time, and more research will be likely to be nearer the exact truth. We must remember this however, that the whole of any truth is never apprehended by one man or in one generation. In the Roman Empire, they used to call a very small section of the earth the world.

The word 'world' to-day means vastly more than it did then. But what they had of it was good and useful for them. But it was only a piece. So it is in regard to the world of mind, and the world of spirit. It is being discovered all the time. The opinions which the men of the past held were not entirely false, they were only partial, crude, and incomplete. We must remember that the duty which Jesus Christ has laid upon us is not to know everything, but to be learners and followers of Him. To follow a person, to get a certain type of character, not to be mentally correct simply, that is what our Lord asks. He asks what *all* can do; His claims are of such a nature that they have universal applicability. Children, young men and maidens, adults and old men, all can follow a person, all can aim at a certain type of character. In a word, all can be Christians. The beginnings of Christian life are very simple, so long as we go to the New Testament; they are complicated and difficult only when man begins to introduce his inventions and confusions into them.

The Church is at one and the same time a school-house; a hospital; a temporary home. But before we can learn what it has to teach, we must be in it. The child enters and then begins to learn. We come into the Church not to display our perfections, for we have none; but to learn about that Kingdom of God of which our Lord spake so much; to learn about ourselves and about God. For, there is nothing on which we seem to exercise our intelligence so lazily as on our own nature and its present needs and future possibilties.

Now when St Paul speaks of our being predestinated or fore-ordained, he is speaking about this nature of ours and what it was made for? He says in effect, that the idea of a thing is in the constitution of the thing itself — but it is also in the mind of God before it is in our mind. Fore-ordination is that to which the thing was ordained before it was actually made. The idea of this building was in the mind of the architect before it was ever put on paper, before it was ever translated into material visibility. And the idea of every part of it was in other minds before it was in his. The idea of Gothic architecture was suggested to the mind of the first man who attempted it, by an avenue of trees, their branches hanging towards each other, forming a peculiar kind of arch. The idea of man and the destiny of man was in the Divine mind before this world was. Man was made according to a divine idea and for a definite purpose. Now, when Jesus Christ comes into the world Paul sees that there is God's idea and purpose for man fully and clearly revealed. And so he begins to speak of that for which man was predestinated; of that for which he was foreordained. His mind is full of it. It does not depress him; it inspires him; animates him, makes life purer and sweeter, grander and more glorious. So much so, that in speaking to the Romans with these ideas of predestination in his mind, he cries out, "If God be for us, who can be against us." Fore-ordination is God *for* us, according to the Apostle. Predestination is God *for* us, according to the Apostle. And there can be no room for doubt that to the mind of St Paul these ideas had nothing in them of gloom or depression. But they have been so used as to bring gloom and depression to many minds. Predestination means purpose. It implies an end. And it implies the provision necessary to carry out that purpose and to accomplish that end. Rightly viewed, it means that the Creator does not work at random, nor blindly, but according to a preconceived idea and along the line of the law which leads up to making that idea into a fact.

In every department of life there is the perfect type. The perfect thing is the complete thing — that which cannot be improved upon. When the Father of our spirits said, "Let us make man" he meant something more by man than you or I mean. He did not mean simply the gardener Adam, nor the herdsman Abraham, nor the smart bargaining man Jacob — the aboriginal Yankee — nor the huntsman Esau, nor the political economist

Joseph, nor the Lawgiver Moses, nor the physically imposing Saul, nor the philosophical Epicurean Solomon, not even the magnanimous David, poet, prophet, king, warrior, saint, sinner, all in one, although David, to our great astonishment is called, " the man after God's own heart." I have no doubt that there are many persons who would be very glad to get those six words out of the record. This poet-king's great sin stands there confessed. Let us remember, that his great repentance stands there confessed, too. There is not a doubt that David was the greatest man of his day, and that in comparison with the men around him he was among the best. He was an all round man, physically, mentally, spiritually. He touched the earth, and he touched the heavens, at more points than any other man of his time. His sympathies were more varied, his nature was larger than any man who then lived. But even this man was not the man God meant. And we do not get to the perfect man until we get to Jesus the Christ. When *he* appears — the very angels of Heaven unite to cry, " Arise, anoint him, for this is He " — this is *the man*.

You and I and all men were predestinated to be according to that type and order. As to the quantity of our manhood, we cannot equal the Man Christ Jesus; as to the quality, we may be like Him. We may be of the same type. And it is the type after all which is the criterion. If we are of the number of those who seek to do the will of God, of the number of those who seek first the Kingdom of God and His righteousness, then we belong to the type of man which the Father of our spirits meant when He said, "Let us make man." I am using scientific rather than theological language because many of our theological terms are worn thread-bare. They are like Saul's armor, which fitted only the man for whom it was made. Or, like some of those coats of mail which I have seen hanging in the baronial halls of old England, very well for the men and methods of the past, but worse than useless for the present. No soldier would think of wearing them in modern warfare. It is of no use our trying to appear respectable in the clothes of our grandfathers, we cannot do it. But the same life which animated them animates us. The same Holy Spirit of God which brooded over their hearts broods over ours. We live on the same earth, but we do not put the vegetables which they grew on our tables. We grow our own. And so we have the same Bible that they had and a better system of exegesis. We can interpret it for ourselves, and in our own methods, and only thus can we, in our generation, be as true to God as they were in theirs. To me predestination speaks of the end which God had in making man, of the type of man that the Creator intended, and of the unchangeable purpose that He has to produce that type — that type, the perfection and consummation of which we have in Jesus the Christ. A man conformed to that type is a man after God's own heart, *not* conformed to it he is breaking away from the destiny which God intended for him.

In the latter part of this passage we are brought face to face with a great truth, contained in the words —" Who worketh all things *according to the counsel of His own will.*" 'Will,' as used in Scripture is always associated with *character*. The Divine will expresses the Divine disposition. We assume often that whatever is done on earth is according to the Divine will, an assumption for which there is no evidence in our Lord's teaching. There is a sense in which we may say that whatever is done on earth He doeth it, for God's laws and decrees are working here all the time. But a judge on the bench may have to commit his own son to prison. He is obliged to do it, or be an unjust judge, and yet it is not according to his will as a father. He is not disposed to do it. His will is not done when that son is sent to jail. And I think that there is no more fruitful source of error and wrong feeling, than the notion that all the pains and sorrows and losses and anxieties and burdens and afflictions of this life are according to God's will. They most assuredly are not. Man's will has vaulted into the place of Sovereignty here on this earth. It has usurped the throne. Man has been trying to do his own will here for these past centuries. He has been persistently refusing to do the will of God. And the results are such as we see. But what then, says one, do you make of the words of the sacred penman, "whom the Lord loveth He chasteneth?" Read on. What follows? "*Not for His pleasure*, but for our profit that we may be partakers of His holiness." It is not acccording to the will of God, to chasten us, but there is no other way to bring us to thoughtfulness and seriousness. And so, this world in which we live does not represent what society would be if the will of God were done. It is a school-house, not a home. It is a place of discipline, not of rest. It is a place where man has to learn a very great deal which is to be useful to him hereafter. But the will of God is not done here, speaking generally; the will of man is. And has been for the centuries past. Everywhere, man is trampling upon God's laws for the body, His laws for the mind, His laws for the heart. Everywhere mercantilism is dominating it over righteousness. Everywhere, those who are sincerely striving to do God's will are in a minority. And they are often last instead of first. But in the eternal future many that are last will be first and many that are first last. Those who are seeking to do God's will here are to be the statesman and prime ministers and leaders when God's Kingdom shall come. How do I know? I know because our Lord told His disciples so. What else can we make of these words, "I appoint unto you a Kingdom, even as my Father appointed unto me, that ye may eat and drink at my table in my Kingdom (perfect fellowship) and ye shall sit on thrones judging the twelve tribes of Israel." These were the representatives of the Jewish race who were doing God's will, and so they were to be the judges and rulers of the nation that was not doing it.

Now, I am persuaded that we often darken our own understandings as to the will of God, by carelessly saying, "It is God's will, I must submit." It is right, it is good to seek resignation; to be brave in the hour of trial, to force down the rebelliousness of our spirits. And yet, to my mind there is more consolation in believing that none of these sufferings and trials are expressive of God's will, that they are the inevitable results of the rebellious will of man asserting itself from generation to generation, until sin and death reign everywhere. God's will is not sickness but health. God's will is not wretchedness but happiness. God's will is not death but life, God's will is not that any should perish but that all should come to repentance, God's will is not hatred, revenge, war, and all the misery these bring. Barbarians may think so, Christians cannot. Judgment is his strange work, mercy is his delight. Jesus Christ revealed God's will. He did God's will. He died to tell us, in the most emphatic way possible, that man's rebellion was the trampling upon holy love; that it was not God's will we should sin and suffer and heap up miseries for ourselves; that the more we do our own wills, irrespective of God, the more we add to the accumulated miseries of our race. Believe this, as you must, if you sit at the feet of Jesus and learn of Him, and the God revealed in Jesus Christ becomes the great attractive centre to which the mind turns, and the accumulated cruelties of the world — its diseases, its malignities, its despotisms — its wars, and all the myriad miseries which afflict it, are man's and not God's. When man separates himself from God, ignores God, and lives self-centred, lives independently of God, lives as though he did not belong to a constitution of things of which God is the centre, he is adding fuel to the fire which the self-willed have already lit; he is storing up for himself, and for others, sorrow and trouble. And then he turns round upon Divine Providence and charges it with his own miseries. He says " God is cruel, God is unkind." Nay; it is man that is cruel, man that is unkind. Our Lord never said, "Beware of God" but "beware of men." We have to be delivered from the tyranny of man, not from God. The tyranny of man over man has been and is something appalling. We call it by various misleading names, that which is proper, that which is the fashion and so on. The simple questions of what is right and what wrong, what is healthy and good, what is the will of God, these are seldom asked. We want to get rid of the pains and penalties of the present and the future, but we are not filled full of the conviction that there is only one way to get rid of them, to find out what is God's will, and do it. When Jesus the Christ was here on earth he said, "I came not to do my own will, but the will of Him that sent me." And the difference between the godly and the godless is here, the one are the willing, the other the wilful. All law and order must rest on some immovable foundation, and there is none to be found but this, the revealed will of God. We are drifting towards anarchy in the family, in the Church and in the nation so long as we magnify individualism and idolize something we call freedom, which with many, means nothing less than anarchy, trampling upon all law and order human and divine, and exalting the will of the creature into supremacy. Those of us who are of the Church of God have to proclaim the exact opposite of this, for we are bound in the same bundle of life with Him whose boast it was " I came not to do my own will, but the will of Him that sent me."

XVIII.

SELF-IMPROVEMENT.

"Take heed to thyself and to thy teaching."—1 *Tim.*, iv: 16.

GENIUS," says a modern writer, "is the passion for self-improvement." While we may be of opinion that this is not an adequate definition, inasmuch as oftentimes we have met with men and women in whom there seemed to be something of that we call genius, without that temper which leads a man to aim at steady self-improvement, yet there is enough of truth in this definition to warrant the affirmation that genius is never effective unless it includes the passion for self-improvement. From a merely human point of view, the Apostle Paul was a man of genius. This man comes before the world with a life as heroic as that which any man ever lived, and a few letters, written, some to churches and two or three to individuals. Yet this life and these letters have immortalized him. Inspiration and genius are not the same thing. The Divine Inspiration wakes the genius into life.

That which is best in any man, that which is most characteristic of him, will arise from its dormancy and latency under the influences of the Spirit of God. Thus, there is in nature room for that beautiful variety of Christian character without which there would be an unedifying monotomy, a tame uniformity in our Christian life. It has been assumed that if a man has genius he does not need to be careful of himself, he does not need to aim at self-improvement. The very opposite is the true state of the case. It is the blood horse that needs the most careful training. "Take heed to thyself" is a word necessary for us all, but it is especially necessary for those of full vitality; for those in whose veins the hot blood seems to course rapidly; for those of highly-strung nervous organization; for those whose impulses are fiery; whose temperament is ardent; whose souls have in them a craving that seems insatiable. If these do not take heed to themselves, there will be disaster. A well-balanced nature, in which the physical, mental, and moral seem to be in happy equilibrium, is not always found, perhaps seldom. Some one department of our organism seems to predominate. The tendency is to cultivate that which it is most easy to cultivate, to the neglect of the other. Consequently, the whole nature is thrown out of balance and a condition of chronic unhappiness is the result.

I want that we should think together this morning of Self-improvement, though the theme seems juvenile; one more fitted for a young men's debating society than for a Christian congregation. We need not, however, be afraid that under the leadership of the Apostle Paul, we shall keep on a level that is unworthy of the most experienced Christian. I would ask you to remark upon the advice which the great Apostle gives to Timothy, one of the earliest presbyters of the Christian Church. Though this man must have had special qualifications for his work, yet these special qualifications did not preclude the necessity for diligent improvement of his mental powers. "Till I come (says the Apostle Paul) give heed to reading, to exhortation, to teaching. Neglect not the gift that is in thee. Take heed to thyself and to thy teaching." He is urged to do everything he can towards self-improvement. On that must depend his usefulness. There is no recognition here of any supernatural grace which would relieve him from the use of those means whereby ordinary men bring their minds into an ability of perceiving what is truth and what error. There are no claims such as that of "Apostolic succession." The man must learn how to use the ordinary opportunities for self-improvement which are within his reach, in order that he may be qualified to do God's work. He must take heed to himself first, or his teaching will not be as full of light and of force as it ought to be.

And so it is with those of us who, in this year of our Lord 1885, are the disciples of Christ, here and now. Not many men have any inward call, or any outward qualification to do public religious teaching. But, not one of us is released from the sweep of this injunction "Take heed unto thyself." Every man of us is a trinity in unity, body, soul, spirit. We have physical, mental and spiritual needs; physical, mental and spiritual abilities — these constitutionally. They are included in the word "manhood." The physical is the pediment on which the mental and spiritual stand. It is that which confines them to this earth. It limits and modifies their use. There is something that we have to learn within these present limitations, which will be useful to us always. Everything must have a beginning, and that beginning has necessarily to be conditioned. For how long our nature is capable of growth we cannot say. What processes it has to pass through before it reaches that condition in which life is blissful receptivity and enjoyment of all around it — of these we are ignorant. But growth is the law of our present state. We soon come to the end of our physical growth; and strange though it seems, very many seem soon to come to the end of their mental growth, although it must be only in seeming. But no one ever comes to the limit of spiritual growth so long as he is on this earth. We seem only to begin that. The most advanced Christian is but a little way on that road, the end of which is perfect accord mentally and affectionally with the mind and heart of our Father in Heaven.

Now, we have to recognize distinctly and clearly that the lower is for the sake of the higher. It is in service to it. The physical is for the sake of the mental, the mental for the sake of the emotional, and all for the sake of the spiritual. There cannot, in the nature of things, be any real self-improvement so long as our ideas on the relation of the lower to the higher are wrong. There is no possibility of any man living the life for which he was predestinated until he apprehends truly something about his own nature. Nor is there any possibility of improvement until that which is uppermost in man constitutionally becomes uppermost in thought. Inadequate views of human nature are at the root of personal miseries and social perplexities. The wise old sage who said, "Know thyself" said more than he knew. The words mean more now than they meant then. Man's view of himself as to what he is and what destined for must affect him beneficially or otherwise in all relations of life and in all that he does. Supposing a man has this view of life, "I am here to be as happy as I can make myself, here to enjoy myself, here simply to have a good time." That is the dominating idea. You see at a glance its limitations. No heroism can ever come out of it; nothing really good or great or sublime. No man moving under the influence of that idea has ever done anything of worth or value. In the olden days they would have called it the Epicurean view of life. Take another view of life, that in which a man sees something to be done out of which comes a material reward. The idea of *duty* dawns upon him, eventually takes possession of him, masters him, and under its influence he denies himself much to which other men are inclined, and becomes the world's successful man in that region concerning which we cannot use any other words than those which convey respect — the commercial. This man becomes stoical. He uses one department of his nature only. He acquires, it may be, that kind of wealth which is represented by money, but he never acquires the ability of using his wealth benevolently so that it will yield the best profit to himself and others. The first man is selfish in one way, and this man is selfish in another way, but he is a better type of man than the first. The Stoic was a better man than the Epicurean.

We might bring other types of men forward in illustration, but these two will suffice. In both cases the nature is depreciated below that for which it was predestinated. Neither man will ever be good or noble. There is no possibility of it. The idea which these men have of manhood and its meaning and purpose is very much lower than God's idea written in the constitution of man. The first man never could be happy and the second man never can be satisfied. Why? Because, in both cases, the nature is larger than the idea which controls and dominates it. Man is unhappy and dissatisfied when his conduct is at war with the upper ranges of his nature. These two men will find entertainment in their several lines. In youth the epicurean style of life has its attractions, even its fascinations; in manhood a life of duty even if there be in it no benevolence, no room for affections and emotions to exercise themselves, yields a certain real satisfaction. But the more humane part of the nature is beggared and hungry. "The eye is not satisfied with seeing, nor the ear with hearing." The spiritual part of man is clamorous. It wants its dues, or its wine turns to venegar; its milk of human kindness to gall. The physical is not here for itself, but for the sake of the mental, the mental is not here for itself, but for the sake of the emotional and the affectional; and the emotional and the affectional are here for the sake of that which is permanent and indestructible in man's nature — the spiritual. As a child cries for its mother so the spiritual in man cries out for its Father, God — "My soul is athirst for God, for the living God, when shall I come and appear before God?" No direr source of misery can ever come to a human soul than to be practically atheistic, for " without God " means " without hope," and hopelessness is the collapse of all that is highest and best in human nature — the total eclipse of the soul. He who makes another man an Atheist has done the cruelest thing of which man is capable. He has blotted out the Sun in the spirit's firmament.

We see then that there is a limit soon reached to physical self-improvement, and a limit also soon reached to improvement arising out of any type or style of life which is dominated by the idea of pleasing one's self simply, or of doing duty which has relation only to that which is seen and temporal. Every man, even the smallest and meanest, is larger constitutionally than his business and larger than his pleasures — using that word as it is ordinarily used. Man's self, what the philosophers would call " *the ego*," is that which needs to be continuously improved. And with its improvement everything else belonging to the man will be raised, will be expanded, will be developed into a higher power. Let the lower nature serve the higher, and the higher will give back to the lower something in return of great value. Everything in a man wakes up when his spiritual nature is awake. If a man be an artist, he is a better artist when his spiritual nature is awakened. The costliest pictures in all Europe are those in which the artists have aimed at bodying forth spiritual themes. It must be so. Pigments and canvass, with brushes and palets, do not make a man an artist. He may be a dealer in colors, like the man at the store who sells them, only on a slightly higher level. But no man ever yet did the highest work of which he is capable till his heart was awake, till the nature began to move and aspire. And the heart will not wake, the spiritual in man will not move in the regions limited by time and sense. Visiting recently the picture galleries of London, there was much that was pleasing, much to excite interest and even wonder, but the most impressive painting even in this matter-of-fact age, is that which cannot be done except under the high inspirations which belong to meditation on Christian themes. Muncacksy's "Calvary" and Holman Hunt's "Triumph of the Innocents"— a fanciful picture representing the souls of the murdered innocents of Bethlehem following Jesus as He is taken to Egypt,— these were the most impressive modern pictures in all London. The child painting in Holman Hunt's picture seems more like the old master's with the freedom and freshness of modern times added. A sum equal to three-hundred and seventy-five thousand dollars was given very recently by the British Government for a religious painting. Artists of all classes never seem to do their utmost and best till the spiritual nature comes into vigorous exercise. And so it is every where. No man is really himself until the spirit within him is awake. The New Testament calls him "dead" till then. It admonishes him in this wise "Awake thou that sleepest and arise from the dead, and Christ shall give thee light." It is all but literally true that a man is never alive until that which is characteristic of him, as man, is alive.

And the distinctive thing in man, that which elevates him above all other creations is, that he can consciously, and of set intent and purpose, worship God. He can anticipate a future, he is so constituted that he can plan and work towards an ideal which fills the imagination, however vivid it may be. No other animate creature can do this. To do this is to act as a man, to do anything less is to fall below the dignity of a man. Self-improvement is, then, the improvement of the spiritual nature.

A type of religious life has been prevalent, we might say dominant, in the past which has almost lost sight of three-fourths of the Pauline theology, anyway of the Pauline ethics. To get a man converted according to the Calvinistic idea of conversion, and then pretty much to leave him as necessarily in a condition of safety, this has been dominant. Conversion means turning the life Christwards instead of turning the back upon Christ and His salvation. But to turn round and stand still is not the Apostolic idea of being a Christian. Any new truth entering the mind brings light, and light means life and life means activity. How is it possible for a man, into whose mind has come the truth of a Redeemer in Christ, into whose heart has come a new love, the love of that Redeemer, how is it possible for him to be the same he was before? To stand and gaze at Christ Jesus is not conversion — to receive Him is. "To them that received Him to them gave He power to become the sons of God." Conversion is the first step in a new and higher life. It is the man claiming that which, in God's ordainment, belongs to him. It is the first step so far as individual choice is concerned to realizing one's manhood. But we do a man harm if we make so much of it that all else is as nothing. The Holy Spirit is a Teacher, "He shall teach you all things." We are at school — learning how to be men and women according to God's idea of men and women. How is our spiritual nature to be developed into more and yet more until it becomes the undisputed sovereign of our constitution? The parable of our necessities is found in the material frame. It can healthfully live only in an atmosphere suited to it. It needs for its nourishment food convenient for it. It needs exercise. So it is with us mentally. So is it spiritually. Christianity is the atmosphere suited to the spirit's life. That spirit needs truth to feed upon. It needs fellowship with other spirits. Whatever promotes faith purifies the soul. Whatever generates hope puts courage into the soul, whatever intensifies affection warms and vitalizes the spirit of man. We know from experience of eighteen hundred and more years that there is nothing in the world which does this like the Christian religion. The best, the strongest, the grandest specimens of manhood have grown up under the inspiration of the facts and truths of Christianity. There are other religions in the world, and I would not deprive men of them if I could not give them something better. It it is better for a man to be chained even to the idea of God as over him than to be without the idea. It is much better to be held to the allegiance we owe to Deity by an attraction which draws our spirits into loving and reverent homage. It is impossible to compel any man to be a Christian because it is impossible to compel love. The heart of man must feel drawn to the object set before it. And so we fail to do any justice to the Christian religion unless its relation to the heart of man be presented so as to wake that heart into response. Along this line all self-improvement must proceed. We must take heed to ourselves.

I venture to add that there is no spiritual self-improvement that is worth anything apart from *plan and purpose*. A spasmodic religiousness will do little. If a young man at college should study only when he feels in the humor he would be disgraced. If a man of business should go to his store or office only when the fit takes him he would be bankrupt. Is it likely that these methods of action will bankrupt men on these lower levels, and save them from bankruptcy on the higher? A spasmodic religiousness without high purpose and intelligent plan is the bane of our time. Spiritual self-improvement means so using the upper regions of our nature as that there shall be development and enlargement of our powers. It means that this should be done in recognition of the fact that we are spirits destined to live on, destined to use hereafter all that here we have acquired of faith and hope and love in a wider and more blessed condition. No material wealth can we take with us hence, but that inward wealth which consists in high aspirations, purified affections, a will consenting to the Divine will, faculty co-ordinated to the needs, services and delights of a condition more glorious than "eye has ever seen or ear ever heard," that we can take with us, that which shall warrant our Lord in saying to us " Thou hast been faithful in a few things, I will make thee ruler over many things — enter thou into the joy of thy Lord."

XIX.

WEARINESS IN WELL-DOING.

And let us not be weary in well-doing; for in due season we shall reap if we faint not — *Galatians*, vi, 9.

THESE words are necessarily addressed to those who are already engaged in well-doing, and who, being so engaged are in danger, of ceasing therefrom because of the weariness which inevitably attends the putting forth of effort of any kind. Weariness may be of three kinds, it may be muscular, or mental, or spiritual. Muscular weariness comes from long continued physical effort; mental weariness from excessive attention to such matters as demand thought; spiritual weariness from loss of faith in a cause, or loss of love to it, or loss of hope of any tangible results. It is to this last kind of weariness that the Apostle refers. It may include the others as nothing worth the doing can be accomplished unless the resources of the mind are expended in the doing of it. Well-doing may be of two kinds, subjective, the doing well to ourselves simply, objective, the doing well towards others. It is quite true that we cannot very well separate these, for as Seneca says, "He that does good to another man does good also unto himself, not only in the consequences, but in the very act of doing it, for the conscience of well-doing is an ample reward." If a man should set himself to improve his mind and manners simply out of a desire to be something better than he had been, he would still, in the doing, be helping others, for he would become a more valuable member of society. And on the other hand, no man can set himself to do good to others without receiving good himself. Hence, it must appear to us that God, in His providence, has so ordered it that well-doing is necessary to well-being. Every one not imbecile wishes well to himself. God has so appointed it that well-doing shall be necessary to the development of the soul to the highest degree of blessedness of which it is capable.

It is assumed, however, that there is a strong temptation to grow weary in well-doing, to cease from good activities; to let opportunities pass unimproved; to allow the best of causes to suffer from want of giving them that assistance which it is competent to us to give.

And this for three reasons. 1. On account of the indolence of our nature. Unless we are tempted to a thing by some immediate pleasure belonging to it, or goaded to it by some stern necessity, there is in us all a tendency to relapse into a condition of indifference and repose. Our physical nature seems to yield readily to the great law of gravitation to which everything material is subject, and oftentimes we too readily obey the lowest of all forces by which we are influenced. To such an extent may we yield to the material part of our being that it becomes tyrannous, the muscles refuse to do their duty readily, the digestion relapses from a healthy tone, and the whole system becomes impaired. And as saintship has, somehow or other, become associated with a pale face, a feeble voice, and general physical incompetence, anyone is at a disadvantage who pleads for health of body as a duty, because of its relation to health of mind and health of soul.

There is the temptation to grow weary in well-doing not only on account of the indolence of our nature but also, 2nd, on account of not seeing adequate results to our efforts. I think that probably this is one of the most general reasons for weariness in the matter of positive well-doing. The man whose mind has been schooled and formed in the commercial world, especially if he has achieved large results in a brief period of time, assumes that he and others ought to have something equally tangible to show for the expenditure of mind and feeling in those directions which are generally included under the words "well-doing." We are constantly hearing of the disappointments which come to all Christian workers; indeed of the discouragements which come to all benevolent helpers of all kinds. We hear far too much of this. Let it be recognized by us that the results of work on mind and heart are not as immediate, certainly not as visible, as the results of work in anything material, and that they require in order to discern them, and estimate them aright, a different order of mind, and that will do something to correct wrong impressions. There is a book published entitled "The History of Humane Progress under Christianity," which ought to be sufficient to help any who read it to take a broader view of this question of results than is generally done. Moreover, no man but he who is unreasonable would ever expect to measure mental and spiritual results by the rules of Arithmetic. Religious statistics are necessary, I suppose, but they are not the less misleading and unreliable. In the olden times Jehovah taught Gideon and David that influence did not depend on numbers. I know how we are all influenced by appearances; we like outsides to be respectable. That does us no harm, so long as we do not substitute appearances for that which is invisible, mind, heart, character. Quality is always more than quantity. I have no doubt that some of the greatest men mentally, and the devoutest spiritually, among the New England clergy of to-day are to be found in villages, ministering to a small handful of people who have not the first approach to an idea of the quality of the man in their pulpit. And that man may be the very type and synonym of faithfulness; *faithfulness*, that which our Lord requires, that about which he always speaks. Nothing else does he ask from any of us than this — to be faithful — faithful to the truth as we see it, faithful to the opportunity he gives, whatever come or do not come from our using that opportunity as well as we can.

I grant you that large results are often given. But the word " results" is a very indefinite kind of word. It may be that the results which God can give are not the results which you mean. " Only one soul brought to Christ by all my efforts," says a discouraged Sunday School teacher. Let us look at that expression a moment. Supposing that Sunday School teacher had built the Pyramids it would have been undeniably a great result of persistent labor, but it would have been such labor as would last at the longest for a limited time, and its use would be problematical, for we are not very sure why and for what the pyramids were built. Supposing one soul is brought to Christ, and permanently united to

Christ by the love and faith of the heart, so united that that soul becomes a faithful Christian soul, living a life of love and faith, doing good to others, and those others doing good to a wider circle still, and so from generation to generation the influence broadens, how can you calculate the result? Admit the Immortality of that soul, follow it beyond the confines of the present, into Eternity; what then? The results are not measured, nor are they measurable. Who has done the greatest work, he who built the pyramids, or that discouraged Sunday School teacher who brought one soul to Christ, into living union with the life-giving Savior? Am I romancing in making such a comparison? Is there anything unreasonable in suggesting that work in that material which we call "mind" and "soul" is essentially different from work on matter? If our Lord could ask the question and yet be reasonable, "what shall it profit a man if he gain the whole world and lose his own soul? If He could put a "soul" against a "world" and appraise it as more valuable, is the comparison we have made illegitimate? Results are not to be estimated by material or arithmetical measurements. In speaking to any who have been engaged in well-doing and have become weary in it, I would rather remind them that our Lord does not put us upon achieving results but upon being faithful to Him and our convictions. If tangible or visible results come, we will be all the more thankful, but if not, the duty of faithfulness still remains. Some results are sure to come. An Apostle who knew what it was to live a martyr's life has left it on record, that no good, honest, Christian work ever yet failed, "Be ye steadfast, unmovable, always abounding in the work of the Lord, forasmuch as ye know that your labor is not in vain in the Lord."

3. And this brings me to a third source of weariness and discouragement in well-doing, our narrow and inadequate views of life. We constantly forget that this life of ours is, as to everything mental and spiritual, the sowing time, not the time of reaping. Evidently this is the thought in the mind of the Apostle, " for, in due season, ye shall reap if ye faint not." The idea of reaping involves the idea of sowing.

When a farmer sows seed he virtually commits it to fructifying influences over which he has no control. He cannot command the sunlight, nor the rain, nor a suitable season for ingathering. He is obliged to trust in a power not his own, and in a beneficence which he calls Nature, but which means God. And so when we sow seeds of truth in a human mind, or the seeds of kindly deeds in human hearts, we commit the seed to God and His Providence. And as the farmer has long patience, so ought we to have long patience. But patience is one of the higher virtues — it is not the same as indifference or laziness, nor is it 'a dogged obstinacy under difficulties' — it is something else than these, the ability to labor and to wait; the ability to stand in face of a mysterious providence, not knowing what it means, or why and wherefore it is sent, and wait those evolvements of life which shall bring the interpretation. The very word "patience" means suffering, for in all wishing and waiting and exploring there is an element of suffering. What a trying time is that which the affectionate watcher by the sick bed has during paroxysms of pain in the sufferer, when no relief can be afforded! If only the watchful eye could see something to be done it would be an immense relief. But to stand by and let pain do its work, this is the trial, this the labor. It is a question in such a case who suffers most, the subject of bodily or of mental pain.

Distributed throughout our life are occasions which bring the need of patience. The soul, needs, for its perfectness, patience as much as it needs anything. And yet, let us not mistake; let us remind ourselves once more that patience is not indifference. Not to care whether life goes this way or that, whether it be good or bad in quality, whether it be spiritual or sensual, whether it end in a blissful immortality or in annihilation, to be perfectly indifferent to all this, that is not patience. It is poverty of mind and heart, want of vitality. To be able to feel even to the point of agony, and yet not to lose hope or heart, to believe on still that through all these sufferings a God, too good to let us live like brutes and die like brutes, is working out something which in the glory of its end shall justify the severity of the means — to hold that attitude of soul against all temptations to abandon it — this is patience.

And so in regard to well-doing, I admit without any debate the impossibility of continued well-doing as a mere matter of policy. Apart from the idea of immortality — apart from the idea of the rewardableness of all well-doing, — persistency in any course which costs self-denial and sacrifice seems to me out of the question. How is it, then, that cases are to be met with of persons who continue in well-doing and yet profess to have no convictions of immortallity for man? We must always make a distinction between that which God has put into human nature, its intuitions, and that which man acquires intellectually. Take, as an illustration of what I mean, the most famous literary woman of this century — her intellect, trained under the influence of a school of philosophical sceptics, became infidel; in the intuitional region of her nature, so far was she from being a sceptic that she was obliged to let herself out in an ode on immortality. Every best character she has drawn is Christian in spirit, self-oblivious, self-sacrificing. All her good sentiments had their roots in that intuitional region which is before and above the intellectual. And so, it is not surprising if sometimes we meet with men and women whose persistent well-doing is not accounted for by their opinions. They have intuitions as well as opinions. Their intuitions are not created by learning or reasoning — their opinions are. A man's opinions belong to the school to which he belongs. The basis intuitions of his nature belong to no school. It is because of this that I believe that when, as is reported, Emerson said to a man who started an argument with him — " I never argue" he acted wisely. When you begin to argue with a man you put him on the defensive. You summon him to do his best to justify himself. It is a simple intellectual contest. Argument has its place and its use, but " convince a man against his will, he's of the same opinion still." Many and many a sceptic is simply the slave of his own opinions, he bends the knee servilely to his own intellectual greatness. It is strange that men are more anxious to appear intellectually strong than morally strong, or spiritually percipient. But so it is. And therefore I would advise those of you who are younger in years than the rest of us, not to be discouraged when you find that you do so very little by the arguments which to you are sufficient if not conclusive. Don't argue. State that which appears to you to be the truth and leave it. If you need a very respectable example to justify you, Emerson in New England is respectable enough, especially with those who are oppressed with the weight of their own culture, or continually living in the enjoyment of a consciousness of being endowed with great intellectual ability. Religion is the development into sovereignty of the intuitions of our nature. To kill them out is impossible. To the end of life they will either trouble us or comfort us. When sceptical men continue in well-doing they but obey their intuitions instead of their opinions. That is the explanation of the phenomenon.

Our narrow views of life account for much of our weariness in well-doing. Practically, we plan for this life and this only. Our sentiments may embrace the beyond, our opinions, actions, plans, purposes are too much controlled by the example set us by the men whose creed is "let us eat and drink, for to-morrow we die." And so we sow only that which we can reap now — or that which the children in our households can reap here on earth. Not entirely of course, but too much.

I do not deny that it is hard, very hard, to continue well-doing in the presence of those mean hostilities which assail every well-doer. In well-doing we have to encounter the want of appreciation of those who have no ability of appreciating anything which has not its origin in themselves; we have to meet all kinds of criticism; we have to be suspected as to the purity of our motives; and not seldom we have to experience the ingratitude of those we try to help; and much else. But, is it not enough for the servant that he be as his Master? These experiences are not new; they do not belong to this generation alone. Our Lord's sinless life was one which provoked every form of hostility that the enemy could bring against it. The troubles of the great Jewish lawgiver began when "it came into his heart to visit his brethren." David lived quietly until God called him into service. Paul was not assailed, but lived in great credit until the Lord summoned him to the preachership of the gospel.

That we are made for doing is evidenced by the ingenious inventions by which men and women kill time, as if the moment we are indolent we are unhappy; that we are made for well-doing is abundantly manifest by the almost countless routes along which we may move towards some end that is in some way beneficent. One cannot contemplate a life like that of the English nobleman whose departure from this earth has been so recently recorded — the late Earl of Shaftesbury — without a sigh at the thought that among that privileged class there was only one such man — a man distinguished by birth, but specially distinguished by his consecration of himself to every kind of benevolence by which he could help others. He did not simply give money but his time — the days and nights as they came, visiting the homes of the poorest and most abject.

When a great orderly crowd of the very poorest and raggedest people in all London assembled outside of Westminster Abbey as the funeral services were held, a man of note, regarding the character of the throng, remarked, "There is not another man in England could gather that crowd." So that human nature, even at its worst, is not all ingratitude. There are so many ways to do good, — and with its usual largeness, Scripture leaves us free to choose our own.

But there is the temptation to forget that the path of active well-doing is the path of allegiance to the Master — of benediction and of growth — that here we are sowing seed whose fifty-fold produce we may never see, but it shall ripen elsewhere. "The due season" may never come on earth. But, in due season, we shall reap that which we sow. That is a just and benevolent law a law that none can escape. I might appeal on the ground of self-interest — only in well-doing can we develop our own natures into the fulness of their powers. To enkindle the mind — to enlarge the heart — to awake the imagination, these will be spiritual results to ourselves, worth while surely. Even here on earth, says Lord Jeffrey, "he will always see the most beauty in things whose affections are warmest and most exercised, whose imagination is the most powerful, and who has most accustomed himself to attend to the objects by which he is surrounded." How are we to get that competence to feel the invisible in the visible which a Wordsworth possessed so royally, which makes Ruskin the high-priest of the beautiful to the age in which he lives? Only by well-doing, not spasmodically and occasionally, but of set intent and purpose. We may, like the caterpillar, spin a very beautiful cocoon and call it our home, but even the caterpillar will teach us, if we will listen, that if he were to remain satisfied in that silken ball which he has woven, it would become not his home, but his tomb. Forcing a way through it, and not resting in it, he finds sunshine and air and life more abundantly. Man says — here will I rest. I will make my home in these pleasant surroundings. I will shut out the sob of sorrow, the wail of the woe-worn, the sigh of the suffering, the baying and babblement of the crowd; here, spending my sympathies on myself, I will enjoy all that is enjoyable. Ah! that silken cocoon! — fastened in it you are dead while you live. No: says God, that is not what I mean for you. And He calls to His aid His angels, clothes them in funeral robes, and they call themselves Pain, Disease, Death; and they stir up the intellect, stir up the heart, stir up the imagination, compel men to think and to feel about Eternity, and then, when it is all over, these disguised angels throw aside the masks they have worn and strip off the sable garb and lo, underneath is the pure white of Immortality. We are sowers of seed here. Let us not forget that he that soweth to the flesh shall of the flesh reap corruption, but he that soweth to the spirit shall of the spirit reap life everlasting. And, "let us not be weary in well-doing, for in due season we shall reap if we faint not."

XX.

THE DIVINE INVISIBILITY.

"Verily, thou art a God that hidest thyself."—*Isaiah*, xlv: 15.

WHEN John the Evangelist wrote "No man hath seen God at any time; the only begotten Son, which is in the bosom of the Father, he hath declared him, (or brought him to view)," he put two great truths into one sentence, the truth of the Divine invisibility, and the truth that man needed to know something definite about Deity. It is impossible for us to account for human life apart from a life-giver. The mind is so made that it demands God. How true it is then that in every nature there is evidence of the existence of a Creator—a Divine Personality! The mind is so made that it also demands that to all worthy action there shall be a reward, and so in every mind there is the truth that God is a rewarder of them that diligently seek Him. Men have tried, with a perseverance worthy of a better cause, to shake themselves free from these ideas, but in vain. Never can we be rid of them till this nature of ours is dissolved into nothingness. Some ideas crush us — such as those of the Infinity and Eternity of the Divine Nature. We can do nothing with them. They are represented to the mind only by vague expanses without any measurement. The wonder is that we can approach them at all. It indicates that our nature is allied to the Divine nature. The thought of the Divine invisibility is not so oppressive as these other ideas, and yet it is perplexing. There are moods in which it is not a welcome thought. It comes to us with no comfort and no help. I suppose that we all have times in which the greater an idea is the more unwelcome it is. We make desperate efforts to put large thoughts away from us, and confine ourselves to that which is measurable and familiar. Yea, have we not often resolved to have nothing to do with that which is unfamiliar, strange, vast, indefinite, awful? Why cannot we live our life in perpetual disregard of everything but the common-place? I suppose that the reason is that in this nature of ours there are possibilities which will not be smothered, intuitions which struggle to get their heads out of the ocean of doubt in which we try to drown them. We have in us from babyhood an irrepressible desire to know the unknown. Tell a child that there is a cupboard into which he must not look, and he will think more of that cupboard than of all the rest of the house. Let there be an apple tree in an orchard whose fruit is forbidden, only one tree in five hundred, and that tree becomes immediately invested with a fascination which is almost painful. There is almost a certainty that the fruit of that tree will ere long be plucked and tasted. Not that which we know but that which to us is unknown, that which is mysterious, only partially revealed, interests us. It appeals to our imagination. We are discontented till we know something of it. The unknown is the awful. And so in heathen religions there is always some mysterious place into which only a high priest enters, some inner sanctuary veiled from mortal eyes where the Divine presence is more perceptible than elsewhere. Even Judaism had it and its veil of the temple was not rent in twain till Christ came. Sacerdotal churches maintain the idea till this day.

Idolatry — what is it? What but the effort to make the invisible visible? There is something pitiful about it. Though its tendency is ever towards materialistic grossness, yet is there something pathetic in it, something more calculated to bring the tear than the frown.

When Jesus the Christ came into this world's life, He came to answer the longing of the human heart after some such expression of Deity as should satisfy that desire to make the invisible visible. Idolatry is the cry of man to God to show himself.

It is the effort of the mind of man to give definiteness to the idea of Deity. In the fulness of time Jesus the Christ comes, and one of His disciples expresses the longing of the whole human race when he cries, " Lord, show us the Father, and it sufficeth us." And when our Lord replies " He that hath seen me hath seen the Father " He but tells us that Almighty God has revealed all that is revealable of his personality in Himself. If only we knew the heart of God we could be satisfied,— anyway, we could have a sort of restful content, and could do our work in the world more hopefully and cheerfully; we could worship with more intelligence — we could work with more confidence.

I think that in our noblest moments it must seem to us that the demand for a full and perfect revelation of Deity is unreasonable, not to use the stronger word, absurd. Reasonable enough is the demand, let us know the *heart* of Deity, the Divine disposition, how God feels towards us. Here we are on an earth that in itself is altogether appalling, because of the material forces which display themselves. We are in the midst of a Providence which buffets us, disappoints us, thwarts and troubles us; a Providence which seems at variance with itself. Reconcile one thing with another we cannot. Generally speaking, most of us seem more to be pitied than envied.

We never know whether we can carry out what we begin. Affliction may come and lay us low, death may come and put the hand of total arrest upon us. We walk by faith because we cannot do ought else. Now, if only we could know that the Infinite Being who sustains and controls all this perplexing and involved condition were as good as He is great, as loving as the best of Fathers to his children, so that if we were suddenly arrested in our life here, it would be a surprise but not a calamity,— would it not make worlds of difference to us? We all feel that it would. And it seems to be reasonable that at the right time in the development of this human race of ours, that demand should be met. It seems to me that it has been met, fully and fairly met, in the gift of Jesus the Christ to this world. And if only we could clear our minds of the prejudices which have been created there by theological and denominational controversies, and look at this Jesus Christ honestly and candidly, it seems to me altogether impossible not to feel that in Him, in what He was and in what He did, is the gospel for humanity, that which every human heart needs.

And so, while it is still true that the Eternal One is a God that hideth Himself, it is also true that the prayer of man's heart "Lord, show us the Father and it sufficeth us," has been answered.

But can we not see that the Divine invisibility has

its uses in the development of this nature of ours? One use is to train us to Reverence. If everything should become so common-place to us that we could treat it with vulgar familiarity, our life would lose its power of self-improvement and development. A thoroughly refined and cultured mind will always see far enough to be abashed in the presence of that which is high and holy. But the vast majority of minds are not refined and cultured. Nor can they be. Think long enough to take in the dreadfulness of the scene — of that coarse, vulgar, hideous mockery which Jesus the Christ experienced in those days which anticipated the Crucifixion. Think of men striking Him, jeering at Him, even spitting in His face, making Him a sham King and I know not what else of coarse, vulgar, shameful conduct. Recognizing what He was — think of it all! Here are men with no ability left to recognize the divine superiority of that unequalled personality. Brutalized Roman soldiers had felt themselves powerless to put a finger on Him because of the unearthliness of His speech, "Never man spake like this man." Lepers had felt new life pulse in them as His shadow fell athwart their path. Fallen women had realized a reviving purity as He spake to them. Devils had trembled in His presence. In this personality there was a mysterious charm, a new kind of power, yet men can sink so low, become so vulgar, so coarse, as to be hideously familiar with such a Presence, and treat it with contempt. Now, there is nothing which so bespeaks meanness of character as the ability to treat things high and holy with contempt. To be capable of respect, of esteem, of affection, is to be capable of that worshipfulness which belongs to God — the witholding of which amounts to treating Deity with contempt. If we could see our natures as they are, with all the possibilities of aspiration and degradation that slumber in them, we should have no sort of doubt that every man needs something to worship more than something to eat. The ability of feeling the splendor, the glory, the beauty of things, and especially the ability to feel the splendor, glory, and beauty in the highest types of human life, this ability indicates a condition of soul in which there is nearness to God. "It is of all things the most melancholy (writes a man entitled to be called great) to watch the moral clouding over of life's early dawn; to trace the dim veil stealing o'er the artless look; to notice how the earnest tone begins to leave the voice, and every worthy enthusiasm dies away into indifference; how it comes to be thought a fine thing to speak coolly of what is odious for its vice, and critically of what is awful for its beauty. Where this spoiling takes place, I believe it is because we mingle no reverence with our affection, and accept without awe the solemn trust of a child's conscience." God hides Himself that we may not become coarsely familiar with that which is Divine and thus add to our sin instead of adding to our Reverence. Further, God's hiding of Himself is necessary to our freedom.

Our Great Teacher puts this thought, as is His wont, into the parable of an Eastern lord going into a far country and delivering his goods into the custody of his servants, that, in his absence, they may so use them as to increase them. In order to the development of every human life, a certain amount of freedom is necessary. The over-awing sensible presence of God would completely destroy our freedom. It would paralyze our activities. It is necessary that men should be from under any fettering constraint if the faculties they possess are to move easily and with spontaneity towards the end for which they were given. Our God is no slaveholder, standing over us with uplifted arm ready to bring down the lash on our palpitating flesh. So much freedom has He given us that it seems to be excessive; oftentimes when crime seems to be here, there, and everywhere even appalling. Not that man is left entirely to himself. Everywhere he meets law, and law means a law-giver. Physically, mentally, morally he is compelled to recognize law, in a word, God as a God of order and not of confusion. But God as law, limiting liberty, and God as Love, inspiring hope, and kindling aspiration, are two different stages in the revelation of Deity. We are all of us anxious to recognize that God is Love, and to rest in it. But our ideas of love and its nature may be very weak, infantile and ignorant. Love is not something that sets law aside. It is not a disposition which indulges a child with all it asks. "Because I love you so, I let you do as you like" — is that the inference proper to love? While the Almighty One has given us that freedom without which our natures cannot develop into strength and beauty,— without which there is no possibility of that variety in which the idea of personality comes out, yet it always seems to me that our freedom is a cord which allows us to go so far and no farther. The most self-willed and reckless of men eventually find that there is a limit to their ability of recklessness. Until we can see the whole area through which the life of the spirit of man moves, I do not believe it possible for us to justify the appalling amount of freedom which God has allowed to His creatures. Still, we can see some of its uses and its necessity. We can see that it gives room for each individual man to show himself. He can choose this or that. By the results of his choice he learns something. He recognizes his mistakes, he feels his error, he builds up his life. He gains experiences which may be of incalculable use to him in the hereafter.

All this suggests itself. But is it not easy to see that if the flaming eye of Deity were visible upon us all the while we should be paralyzed into inaction? Our rightful freedom makes the demand upon God that He hide Himself from our vision. *Moreover it is necessary to our perfectness of nature.* There must be a limit to the growth of this nature of ours, a point attainable at which, in every moment of our existence, we shall feel like praising God for our creation. There must be for man a state of life which is itself bliss — harmony — music, in which the internal and external are in accord. *Now* we live by effort, by endurance, by overcoming difficulties, by braving dangers, by surmounting obstacles, by resisting evils. It is a kind of chronic warfare with men and things.

But in us are ideas of something entirely different and immeasurably superior. Those ideas are endorsed by Jesus the Christ. But perfectness in man is not simply a matter of outward condition, it implies internal correspondence with an enviroment in itself perfect. In order to perfectness of inward condition there must be the ability of faith in a Power outside ourselves, and of faith in all around us, the ability of perpetual hope, the ability of undying love. It is not possible for us to conceive of a state in which these three elements of life will not be needed. And it is not possible, so far as we can see, to develop these virtues unless we have room for their growth. The invisibility of God is necessary to their growth. Sight is very much inferior to trust. The most perfect communion of soul with soul, the most exquisite fellowship of mind with mind, are possible only where undoubted trust and undying love are possible, nowhere else. Now, if our God were to show Himself as over us, watching us, noting us all the time, every day and every hour, so that the eye saw Him, would we not feel as the slave feels when the Master is there whip in hand? If the Almighty One were simply an Almighty Taskmaster, or an Almighty Detective, what possible room would there be for the growth of these three royal virtues, faith, hope and love? But now He hides Himself, conceals His presence and His workings, so that we have to bring faith into exercise. And nothing so ennobles and purifies a spirit as the exercise of faith in somebody. The opposite of faith is fear and suspicion. Train a child under the influence of these and see what the result will be. Nothing good, a blight will be on that child's soul for life. There are some men who need watching all the time. If you employ them and are to get any work out of them you must keep an eye on them. Of what order are these men? The very lowest to be found anywhere. Nothing noble in them.

And yet, though God hides Himself and refuses to be the Supreme Detective of the Universe, He fills Heaven and Earth. He is never absent. We cannot get away from Him. We cannot escape Him. He hides Himself, in the presentative totality of His Being, but He does not hide all His *thoughts*. Every material thing is a thought of God presented to us for our recognition. It used to be assumed that man would become unspiritual if he admired Nature, the heavens, the earth, the cattle on a thousand hills, the birds, the flowers. No man, with a Bible in his hand ought to have felt so. How full of poetry is the Bible! It sings its highest revelations. And the more spiritual in mind we become, the more certainly shall we find "sermons in stones, books in the running brooks, and God in everything." Nature is a library of Divine thoughts to the spiritualized mind, to no other mind,— thoughts presented in forms of beauty, put there for us to find them. You know how children like to discover things, and so we are put upon discovering Divine thoughts. They are spoken to us in parables. These are everywhere, and what we call our discoveries are simply the wider opening of our eyes to see what was there all the time. "All our boasted discoveries are only of things that for thousands of years have stared us in the face and we could not recognize them. We must marvel rather at the tardiness than the swiftness of our apprehension and confess ourselves but fools and slow of heart to perceive what the finger of God has plainly writ."

But not His thoughts only has God spread out before us. He has made us feel His *feeling*. He has put fatherhood and motherhood into men and women. He has put sisterhood and brotherhood also. He has made souls capable of friendship. He has put pity, compassion, sympathy, love into human hearts. And though these are necessarily adulterated, yet there is much of the genuine article to be found. All these have to be accounted for. They are not in the dust out of which our bodies are made. It is next to impossible to believe that any man is serious when he talks as if pity and sympathy, compassion and love and all these elements of moral beauty are the result of "a fortuitous concourse of atoms."

For myself, I don't care whether the physical nature of man was, by what we know as the method of evolution, developed from the lower and the lowest, or whether, by some more summary process, it was created. It is the *result* not the *process* with which we are concerned. It is interesting to know how the rocks were stratified, how the hills were cast up, how the valleys were ploughed. But the result rather than the process concerns me. I can plant potatoes on the hills;

I can graze cattle in the valleys. I can train my mind to a feeling of the beautiful by the undulating variety all around. And so this organism of ours may have come up from those other creatures with four pillars to support their frame, instead of two. The vertical man may once have been physically the horizontal animal. It makes no difference as to the process. Now he is *man* — capable of love, of pity, of sympathy, of compassion, and these are not animal. They are the Divine feelings reproducing themselves in the creatures prepared to incarnate them. And though God hides His Infinite Personality, draws around Himself a veil which none can rend — we know some of His thoughts, and some of His feelings. His whisper is in our souls. We name it conscience. He never leaves us, nor forsakes us. And, with the Hebrew poet we can ask, "Whither shall I go from Thy spirit — whither shall I flee from Thy presence? If I ascend up into Heaven, thou art there; if I make my bed in Sheol, behold thou art there. If I take the wings of the morning and dwell in the uttermost parts of the sea; even there shall thy hand lead me and thy right hand shall hold me."

And with Paul, "In Him we live and move and have our being." And when we come to Jesus the Christ, the veil of concealment is so thin that we can see through it. Are we too rash when we say — Deity reduced from His Infinity, coming within limitations such as we need on this earth would be Perfect Humanity? Wonderful language is *that* " know ye not that ye are temples of the Holy Spirit." Man regenerated is the true temple, and at the inmost of every regenerated human soul is a ray from the Central Sun of the Universe — God Himself. Thus God is hidden, yet manifest. And so, though God hides Himself from us, we cannot hide ourselves from Him. " Can any hide himself in secret places that I should not see him, saith the Lord; do not I fill Heaven and Earth, saith the Lord?" Here, even here, is the ground of our hope and expectation. The touch of God is everywhere — beyond it we cannot go.

www.ingramcontent.com/pod-product-compliance
Lightning Source LLC
Chambersburg PA
CBHW032054220426
43664CB00008B/1001